KENTUCKY DERBY
STORIES

Secretariat, the 1973 Triple Crown champion, at Claiborne Farm in 1974. (Courtesy Dick Martin, Louisville, Kentucky)

KENTUCKY DERBY
STORIES
Jim Bolus

PELICAN PUBLISHING COMPANY
Gretna 1993

The word "Pelican" and the depiction of a pelican are
trademarks of Pelican Publishing Company, Inc., and are
registered in the U.S. Patent and Trademark Office.

Library of Congress Cataloging-in-Publication Data

Bolus, Jim.
    Kentucky Derby Stories / Jim Bolus.
      p. cm.
    ISBN 0–88289–984–8
    1. Kentucky Derby, Louisville, Ky.—Anecdotes. I. Title.
  SF357.K4B63   1993
798.4'009769'44—dc20   92–36082
                                             CIP

*The words "Churchill Downs," the "Kentucky Derby,"
and the replication of the "Twin Spires" are registered
trademarks of Churchill Downs, Inc., and are used
herein with the permission of Churchill Downs.*

*Jacket photo courtesy of Dick Martin, Louisville,
Kentucky*

Manufactured in the United States of America
Published by Pelican Publishing Company, Inc.
1101 Monroe Street, Gretna, Louisiana 70053

To my children,
Bo and Jen . . .
two special people.

Contents

Acknowledgments

First and foremost, I wish to acknowledge my indebtedness to Judy Bortner, director of retail operations for the Kentucky Derby Museum. Without her suggesting my name to Pelican Publishing Company, this book would never have gotten off and running.

Special thanks also go to head librarian Doris Waren and associate librarian Cathy Schenck at the Keeneland Library. They have always been my right hand in researching horse racing.

I also thank the entire staffs at Churchill Downs and the Kentucky Derby Museum, as well as the New York Racing Association press office.

Books that have served as research sources include *Run for the Roses, The Kentucky Derby Diamond Jubilee, The History and Romance of the Horse*, and *A Sound of Horses*.

Many publications have been used through the years in researching the chapters that appear in this book, including *The Courier-Journal, The Blood-Horse* magazine, and *Daily Racing Form*, as well as such now-defunct publications as *The Thoroughbred Record* (formerly the *Kentucky Live Stock Record* and later the *Live Stock Record*), *The Louisville Times, The Louisville Commercial, The Spirit of the Times*, and the *Goodwin's, Krik's*, and *Watson's* racing guides.

For photographs, I wish to thank Amy Petit at the Keeneland Association, Debbie Blair and Jamie Miller at the

Breeders' Cup, Andy Belfiore at the New York Racing Association, Benoit & Associates, and longtime friend Dick Martin.

Hundreds of people have assisted me and been patient with me over the years, and there isn't enough space to list them all. But three people who deserve sincere acknowledgments are Billy Reed, a friend and writer with whom I have shared many Derby experiences; the late Mike Barry, who taught me so much about this grand old race; and Joe Hirsch, who is directly responsible for my interest in the Derby's history.

Introduction

When Col. M. Lewis Clark founded the Kentucky Derby, he foresaw greatness for the race. True to his forecast, the Derby started off in impressive fashion for the first decade or so, but then it went into a slump, and when Colonel Clark died in 1899, a suicide victim, the race was struggling. Little did he know that the Derby would be rejuvenated, that it would become a world-famous spectacle, that it would be hailed as "the greatest two minutes in sports."

Thanks to the foundation laid by Colonel Clark, and the subsequent promotional work of Col. Matt Winn, the Derby today stands tall as the most important horse race in America, perhaps in all the world.

In trying to put together a book on the favorite Kentucky Derby stories that I have written over the years, I naturally resurrected pieces that I had done on Colonel Clark and Colonel Winn. To tie in a modern-day figure at Churchill Downs, I've included a story on Warner L. Jones Jr., a director at the historic track since 1941. When Jones became a director, Colonel Winn was Churchill Downs' track president. Colonel Winn saw the first seventy-five Derbies—from the first in 1875 through the Diamond Jubilee in 1949. Jones is a great-great-great nephew of Colonel Clark and an admirer of Colonel Winn. Those three Kentuckians—Col. M. Lewis Clark, Col. Matt Winn, and

Warner L. Jones Jr.—are linked together from the Derby's very beginning to today.

Another person who loved the Derby was Mike Barry, a Louisville newspaperman who attended his first running of this race as a youth in 1922. Mike saw sixty-six Derbies altogether until his death in 1992. Mike was a great friend of the Derby—and a great friend of mine. We stood side by side in the Downs press box to watch many Derbies. After Genuine Risk won the 1980 Derby, we both applauded her as she was led to the winner's circle, and we enthusiastically shook hands. We had just witnessed one of the race's priceless moments: a filly had won the Derby, and we very much appreciated being on hand to witness the event.

Mike was a crutch that I relied on for information, for encouragement, for support. The Derby will never have a bigger fan than Mike Barry, and I thought that a story on his letters back home to the *Kentucky Irish American* during World War II best illustrated where his thoughts were when the Derby would roll around during those years.

One of my favorite horses was Dancer's Image, and he leads off a chapter entitled "A Touch of the Derby in the Orient." On my first visit to Japan in 1987, I went to that country's thoroughbred breeding center on the island of Hokkaido and saw Dancer's Image. It was nineteen years after he had crossed the finish line first in the 1968 Derby. As a twenty-five-year-old newspaperman in '68, I had written about Dancer's Image at the Derby, one of the biggest stories I ever covered. Then, nineteen years later, I was paying him a visit. I thought about Peter Fuller, his former owner, and so many others who used to cheer his stretch charges. I felt that any number of this horse's fans back in the United States would love to have traded places with me on this trip to Hokkaido. Just seeing Dancer's Image was easily the highlight of that visit to the Orient.

Other chapters that I've included deal with such topics as the black jockey era, a fascinating subject worthy of a book itself; second-stringers who've run well in the Derby, proof that this race is so very unpredictable; close finishes that likely would give you heart failure if you watched a Derby highlight film of every thrilling stretch battle; and races involving Derby winners.

Another chapter is devoted to celebrities. Colonel Winn knew the importance of bringing celebrities to the Derby, and a few of these show-business types have come to Louisville with a Derby starter. These celebrities with Derby candidates make a good story, and I've been fortunate enough to share some experiences with Telly Savalas and Jack Klugman.

And then there's a chapter on the worst horses to run in the Derby. Why the worst? Why not the best? Those are good questions. Here's a good answer: my record at picking the Derby winners is not very good. I average one Derby winner every ten years—Pleasant Colony in 1981, Strike the Gold in 1991. I tell everybody to check with me in the twenty-first century for my next Derby winner. The point that I'm trying to make is that I'm much better at picking bad horses than good horses. Surely, I've bet on enough losers in my lifetime to know a bad horse when I see one. I can't guarantee anybody a winner at the races, but I'll stack my "Dirty Dozen" against anybody else's list, and I'll bet my life that my twelve Derby starters are tons the worst. So I, better than anyone else, should dishonor these plugs with a chapter about their futility and failures and frustrations. (Besides, it's a lot more fun writing about the worst Derby starters than the best.)

There are other chapters in this book. Nobody has ever succeeded in putting into words what the Derby is all about, and this book doesn't pretend to tell the story of the race from beginning to end. It's just a collection of my favorite stories about my favorite sporting event—the Kentucky Derby. I've always enjoyed researching the Derby and writing about the old race. I hope that you enjoy reading about it.

KENTUCKY DERBY
STORIES

For years, this photograph of Mike Barry appeared with his column in the Kentucky Irish American, *a popular weekly newspaper. The heading over the photograph referred to Mike as the "world's greatest handicapper at work." (Courtesy* Kentucky Irish American)

1

Mike Barry's Wartime Recollections of the Derby

LONGTIME LOUISVILLE NEWSPAPERMAN Mike Barry spent four years in the service, far away from one of the loves of his life . . . the Kentucky Derby.

In 1942 and 1943, he was in Florida at Derby time. In 1944, he was in Hawaii. In 1945, he was in Okinawa. During his two years in the Pacific, he was an Army Air Corps captain attached to the 292 Joint Assault Signal Corps Operation, 77th Cavalry.

Barry may have been thousands of miles away from home, but when the first Saturday in May rolled around (or, in 1945, when early June came along), his heart was at Churchill Downs, a track he was first introduced to as a youngster.

Barry saw his first Derby as a twelve-year-old in 1922.

Morvich, the unbeaten two-year-old standout of the previous season, was heavily favored to win the '22 Derby. The speedy colt went to the lead at the start, and Mike, observing the race from the infield, had an opinion. He was a smart-aleck kid, that young Mike Barry, and he had the audacity to say of the heralded Morvich: "He'll never last!"

Here the horses hadn't run a quarter of a mile, and Barry was already wrong.

Looking back on that race years later, Barry would write: "I've always thought of it as an omen. Anybody who

Mike Barry with his wife, Bennie, at Churchill Downs. (Courtesy Jim Bolus)

could be so spectacularly wrong in his first Derby predic-
tion was obviously destined for a long, full life. Full of
losers."

Well, Mike Barry did live a long, full life. He picked
plenty of losers, but don't let anybody kid you. He had his
share of winners, too.

The dean of Kentucky Derby writers, Barry saw sixty-six
runnings of this world-famous race, many of them from the
press box as first a writer for the *Kentucky Irish American*,
then *The Louisville Times* and, later in retirement, as sec-
retary-treasurer of the National Turf Writers Association.

Unlike many writers, Barry knew what he saw when he
witnessed the Derby. He didn't merely observe the race; he
actually *saw* what happened.

Barry died on January 10, 1992, at the age of eighty-two
and took with him a library of Derby memories.

Lively, witty, opinionated, quite knowledgeable, and always young at heart, Barry was a colorful writer. During
World War II, he would write letters back home, letters
that would appear in his family-owned *Kentucky Irish American*, and when it was time for the Run for the Roses at
Churchill Downs, you could tell by his correspondence
that he had a bad case of "Derby fever," even though he
was far, far from his ol' Kentucky home. Join us as we go
back through the war years with this "smart-aleck" kid and
share his comments on the Derby:

1942—Barry saw twenty straight runnings of the Derby
until Uncle Sam made him an offer he couldn't refuse. For
the 1942 Derby (and the next three years), Barry was in
the service. Even so, the *Kentucky Irish American* would
carry comments from Mike and his other brothers who
were in the service.

Under a column headlined "Brothers In Arms," Barry
wrote after the Derby: "You know, last Saturday afternoon, I hadda have a radio, one I could carry around. I

borrowed a set small enough to hide under the bulge in my form-fitting shirt so I wouldn't have to march around uniformed but uninformed.

"The set was plenty little, but was it loud! However, it was just an unfortunate coincidence that my favorite program came on the air right in the middle of the colonel's speech.

"I say it was coincidence.

"He says it was sabotage.

"Who's the jury gonna believe?

"I don't know, but if you wanna bet on me you can sure get big odds.

"There we were, a thousand strong and me in the shape I'm in, lined up in long rows on the field. We were all supposed to be standing at attention listening to the colonel's regular weekly pep talk, but hidden back in the ranks a lone private fiddled desperately with dials and knobs on a radio.

"I needn't tell you the name of that private. He's still a lone private, too. There's ain't another soul in this dungeon.

"After hours of warm-up growling, the colonel reached the climax of his windy monolog. 'Men,' cried this old rabblerouser from way back, 'we must be ready for anything! As we stand here, what earth-shaking events are happening at this very moment?'

"He paused for dramatic effect, and the silence of the grave hung over the field—but only for a moment.

"Just as the colonel inhaled to ask again, in 35-cent words, what was cooking, he got an answer. In a roar they must've heard in Key West, a voice rang out:

"'ALSAB'S MOVING UP!'

"The voice was the voice of Clem McCarthy, but the hand that turned the dial was mine. I also have title to the body that's wasting away on a steady diet of bread and water.

"They are pretty lenient, though. I get my choice of bread—white, rye or whole wheat.

"The only thing I really mind is the lack of information. I am burning with curiosity—that one flash about Alsab is all I heard of the Derby broadcast.

"Of course that was enough, but I would like to know for sure just how far he won by and what he paid.

"If Alsab paid more than $3.20 to win it was a steal, because he looked to me like the biggest cinch that ever ran for the roses.

"I am also a little curious as to who finished second and third. Devil Diver and Apache, probably, just the way I picked 'em. Boy, naming 'em 1–2–3 is really snapping out of an eight-year slump!

"I certainly laughed last week at those pre-Derby stories about Eddie Arcaro being unable to decide whether to ride either Devil Diver or Shut Out.

"After all it really didn't make any difference—neither one of 'em had a chance against Alsab—but I thought Arcaro was smarter'n that. The dumbest horseplayer in the world could tell him to pick Devil Diver. I could tell him!

"Just why he was in doubt is something I'll never figure out. How in the world could he consider a bum like Shut Out? This turtle's a son of Equipoise, and you know how I always told you every one of Ekky's children was a sprinter. You couldn't drag Shut Out a mile and a quarter!

"Some dopes just never will learn about horses, I guess."
NOTE: The real dope on the '42 Derby finish was that Alsab may have been moving up, but not fast enough. He finished second to that bum Shut Out.

1943—By now, four Barry brothers (Mike, Joe, Dan, and Tom) were contributing to the "Brothers In Arms" column.

"When I missed the Derby last year," Mike wrote back home to his brother Jim, "I swore a sacred gypsy oath that nothing or nobody would keep me away in 1943. Brother, never trust a gypsy.

"This is 1943, and I'm away, away, away down south in Dixie, where even the traffic signs read 'No U-all Turns!'

"For my money, the Fleet's in. I think the Count will win 'by hisself,' with Ocean Wave nosing out Blue Swords for what's left, and you may quote me.

* * *

"My conscience hurts me.

"You know what a conscience is—that still, small voice telling you somebody's looking. I'm hearing loud voices, and I know somebody's looking.

"The voices are from the men in this camp, and they're looking for the guy who posted a notice on the bulletin board last Saturday morning, to wit:

"'Count Fleet has a broken leg and will not start in the Kentucky Derby. Positively.'

"By a strange coincidence, the only guy on the post who didn't believe what he read was me, and when I walked around saying Count Fleet was a cinch I found quite a few greedy warriors offering to bet me the Count wasn't.

"They talked me into it, brother. I bet them he'd win, and I made a lot of bets on the Count, all at even money. You people at the track only got 2 to 5, but I got even money.

"That's why my conscience is bothering me.

"I shoulda made 'em give me odds.

* * *

"No fooling, brother, I clipped more guys in this place than the post barber, although of course not quite so close. It was one of those things you dream about.

"I've been a lot of places in this fair land of ours, and everywhere I found people who had heard of the Kentucky

Derby, but right there their knowledge stops. These peasants in the provinces don't know the distance, the entries, the odds, or anything.

"Especially they don't know the odds. 'You mean you'll take Count Fleet against the field?'

"'That's right,' I'd say, looking as stupid as possible. 'How much d'ya want?'

"'You mean I get all the rest of the horses?' he'd say. "'Every one of 'em,' I'd say, 'including the lead pony.'

* * *

"That got him. Out would come the old folding money, down would go his name in my book, and then I'd hustle him along to make way for the rest of the line.

"Once in a while I'd find a cautious customer who'd want to know the names of the other horses, so I'd give him the whole list.

"Oh well, anybody can make a mistake. However, I do feel a little bad about one five-buck contributor. How or why I did it I don't know, but when I saw that lovely fin I couldn't resist.

"I gave him Man o' War.

* * *

"The colonel's a good loser, though. Everybody says so, and I'm sure I'll be out of the guardhouse in no time at all.

"It wasn't a measly five dollars that made him mad. When he talked to me he didn't mention the money, but he certainly covered the rest of the ground pretty thoroughly.

"'You,' he said, 'you! When you started writing "P.S. Count Fleet is money from home," on official correspondence I let it pass. When you nailed a horseshoe to a P-40 and punctured the gas tank I just called it one of the horrors of war. When you yelled "They're on the track!" right after the bugler sounded Retreat I prayed for strength.

"'Those things I could stand. After a year with you I thought I could stand anything, but now I know I can't. This afternoon you went too far.'

"'Too far?' I said. 'Too far? Nonsense, sir—only a mile and a quarter, and the Count can run all day . . .'

"'Quiet!' he roared. 'Not that blasted horse! You're the one who went too far! I didn't like those binoculars slung around your neck, and that checkered vest and two-tone brown-and-white shoes are both non-reg, but when you started screaming "Katy bar the door!" over the public address system the guards thought the field was being attacked and sounded the alarm!'

"A busy little bee, wasn't I?

* * *

"I'm planning to be home next week to help Brother Dan acquire a new commanding officer, but there'd better not be any delay at the altar. Best man or no best man, that first post time at Churchill Downs don't wait for nobody." *NOTE: Count Fleet won the '43 Derby by three lengths and went on to sweep the Triple Crown. As for Man o' War, he wasn't eligible for the Derby in 1943. It seems that at that particular time of his life, he was twenty-six years old . . . and standing at stud at Faraway Farm.*

1944—This year there were five Barrys in the "Brothers In Arms" column, Jim joining the other four.

With a dateline of "Somewhere in the Pacific," Mike wrote a letter that appeared in the May 13 issue:

"News reaches us in maddening, disjointed scraps. Today is Sunday, April 23, and through my secret agents I have discovered Stir Up won the first division of the Wood Memorial yesterday. Broad Grin ran third and Pukka Gin finished fourth, 6 1/2 lengths back. I am also informed that Lucky Draw won the second division of the Wood.

Who ran second to Stir Up? Who ran second and third to Lucky Draw?

"For all I know, it could have been Margo G. and Butter Beans.

"By the time this reaches you, the Derby may be history, and by the time I find out who won he'll probably be a 4-year-old. Anyway, X-9 just decoded a flash that said Platter was scratched, so I am a man without a horse. Pending last-minute word from me, I'll take Count Fleet right back."

In the May 20 issue, he wrote that he had "just listened to the running of the seventieth Derby, the third since our war began and the third I've missed in twenty-three years.

"We have a public address system set up in our area, over which we broadcast official announcements, music, news, etc. I suggested to the officer in charge that we hook up a radio and carry the running of the classic.

"'I don't know,' he said. 'Is it of general interest?'

"He gets a military funeral Monday.

"Our time is four and a half hours behind Louisville time, and both Hawaii stations carried the running from twelve-thirty to one o'clock. In the pool on the race I drew Gay Bit, and I'm still not sure he didn't win. The last I heard he was in a photo finish with Pensive and Gillette Blue Blades.

"We had no choice other than to listen to Ted Husing. This was better than no broadcast at all, but not much better."
NOTE: Pensive won the 1944 Derby by four and a half lengths. It turned out that Gay Bit, a 25–1 shot, finished sixth.

As for Gillette Blue Blades, a mystery has surfaced. A check with the names department at The Jockey Club uncovered the fact that no horse has ever been given the name of Gillette Blue Blades. After informing us of that fact, the woman at the registry intoned, "Look sharp . . . feel sharp . . . be sharp . . ."

Hmmm. Methinks she must be a lot sharper than we are.

1945—The Derby traditionally is held on the first Saturday in May, but in 1945 it wasn't run until June 9 because of a wartime ban on racing in the United States lasting for four months until V-E Day on May 8.

From Okinawa on June 12, 1945, Barry wrote:

"Sunday I heard my fourth consecutive Derby by radio, and I'm determined not to run that string to five. I'm going to have this war over before next May if I have to start fighting myself. Boy, am I desperate.

"I was in Florida in '42 and '43, Hawaii in '44, and now Okinawa in '45. My plans for 1946 are already under way. I am getting comprehensive reports from my underground guerrilla forces in Louisville, who at great risk to their own bankrolls made a thorough reconnaissance of the proposed invasion point, namely Churchill Downs.

"Next year I'm not going to fritter away my strength in costly frontal assaults. Not after the education I've had in flank movements. I trust the regular patrons at the Downs will not be too surprised when they see me wriggling around behind the sellers windows, then throwing a grenade and charging the last few feet.

"Just a smoke grenade, of course. I figure this will also hide me from the distressed dowagers who always manage to get in front of me, then buy a piece of the horse I've just spent hours scientifically handicapping. In a fit of rage, I play something else.

"Not that it makes any difference. They both lose.

* * *

"This year the radio service was none too good—they're always cluttering up the air with a lot of this silly war news—and I was unable to get advance notice of the Derby broadcast until the day before, when Radio Okinawa announced they would rebroadcast the race at 12:15 Sunday. (The Derby was actually run early Sunday morning, our time.) Once committed, Radio Okinawa just couldn't quit, and all day long kept reminding listeners not to miss the Derby at 12:15 Sunday.

"Sunday at 12:15 we're all gathered around the radio, and dear old R.O. says the time has been changed to 7:15 Sunday night. At 7:15 they gave the 1–2–3 finish—that's all. Had I depended on this station it would no longer be on the air. Not while I had a shot left.

"However, Sunday afternoon I got a short-wave receiver and picked up one of the numerous rebroadcasts just at the point where the field had reached the starting gate, and so heard the complete running. Ted Husing called it, which was better than no broadcast at all.

"But not much better.

*   *   *

"In a blurred broadcast the day before, I picked up the starting field in order of post positions, and sold 16 chances at ten yen each. As the promoter, I naturally drew a strong contender—Misweet. One filly in seventy years, and I get Misweet.

"The names were so hard to distinguish I expected to be charged with obtaining money under false pretenses, but nobody complained. For example, I sold Bert G. as Bert Lahr, Hoop Jr., as Hook Jr., and Sea Swallow as Be Fearless. If Sea Swallow had won it would have been Katy-bar-the-door. The holder of Be Fearless would still be looking for 160 yen.

"The Major drew Pot o'Luck, and after a whispered conference in which I informed him this was Ben Jones' charge and a strong contender, he made individual horse-for-horse bets with all the other officers. Naturally I told them Pot o'Luck couldn't beat a fat man kicking a barrel around the track, so the Major had no trouble lining up takers. You can see I know which side my Spam's fried on.

"Two officers didn't bet the Major. I wouldn't bet Misweet against anybody except Kenilworth Lad—I told the fellows I'd never heard of him but any horse with a name like that was sure to run last. Obviously I haven't lost all of my old skill.

"The other was the guy who held Hoop Jr., and you know why the Major wouldn't bet against him? He didn't know Hoop Jr. from Adam's off ox, but he refused to wager against a horse owned by a fellow Floridian.

"That beat me. It beat all the others, too, and you should have seen the long unsmiling line in front of his tent Sunday night. He won a hundred and forty yen. Boy, what a killing! Oh yeah, that's fourteen bucks American.

"By the way, where did Adam's off ox finish? Tab for later—been working awfully well lately."

NOTE: Regret, the first filly to win the Derby (1915), didn't have to move over and make room for Misweet, who finished twelfth in the '45 Derby. As for Kenilworth Lad, he was beaten eight lengths—by the next-to-last horse, that is. All told, Kenilworth Lad finished fifty-two lengths behind Hoop Jr.

1948—Barry didn't forget his experience in the service. In the spring of this year, he wrote that he had "often considered suing the government for four or five thousand dollars on account" of the 1942 Suburban Handicap.

"Market Wise, my favorite charger, paid better than 4 to 1, but instead of staging a clean-up that would have made Pittsburgh Phil's biggest seem like two cherries and a lemon on a slot machine, I wasn't aboard for a dime.

"That particular afternoon I was confined to a hotel room in Miami Beach, while a desperate nation struggled desperately to make an officer out of me. Things, as you see, were desperate. I've often thought of the money we both would have saved if they'd turned me loose, but they wouldn't. The standards of OCS, I was told in stern fashion, did not permit candidates to throw away field manuals and head for handbooks. They were pretty stiff-necked in those days.

"Oh well, I guess everybody suffered in the war. A few, perhaps, more than I did, although I'm still difficult to convince. . . ."

One Final Word . . .

Barry was the dean of Kentucky Derby writers, and in 1991 he saw his sixty-sixth running of the Churchill Downs classic. Writing for *The New Voice*, a weekly newspaper in Saint Matthews, Kentucky, he made his Derby predictions, and, in a headline size usually reserved for the outbreak of world wars, readers saw his selection in big, bold letters: **"Mike Barry picks Strike the Gold."**

Barry, who was wrong on his first Derby in 1922, was right on his last one in 1991. Not only did he pick the winner, but he also selected the second-place finisher— Best Pal.

Writing in the *1989 Kentucky Derby Magazine*, Barry offered these sage tips for those who like to wager on the races:

"WORKOUTS. Yes, sir, check those workouts. You've got to believe in those published workout times just as firmly as you do in Santa Claus, the Easter Bunny and those letters from publishers saying you're about to win $10 million, maybe $20 million. All you've got to do . . .

"At last count there were 43,196 children walking the streets of New York alone, hungry and barefoot, all because their parents believed in workouts.

"HUNCHES. Racetrackers like to say, 'Get a hunch and bet a bunch.' They never add the next line, which is 'and all next week you'll eat no lunch.' Just bear in mind the man who was watching the horses leaving the paddock and happened to see a priest making a sign with his hands as one horse walked by. He rushed to the window and bet all he had.

"His horse never ran a yard, dropping back at the start and finishing a dead last. On his way back to the paddock the man saw the priest. 'What happened, Father, what happened? I saw you blessing that horse, and what more heavenly guidance did a good Catholic need?'

"'A fine Catholic you are,' the priest said. 'You don't know the difference between a blessing and the last rites.'

"PRAYER. An owner once told me, 'I always pray before a race, but I don't pray to win. I just ask for heavenly help to take care of my horse and the rider, pray that all the horses and all the riders have a safe journey, things like that.'

"I saw this owner the next day. 'Now that I watched your horse yesterday,' I said, 'I believe you ought to make a change. Next time, pray for him to win.'"

NOTE: *Barry always had a favorite prayer himself at the race-track:* "*Dear Lord, please help me to break even today. I can use the money.*"

2

Down to the Wire

THE KENTUCKY DERBY is hailed as "the greatest two minutes in sports." It's called "a mile and a quarter without any water," meaning that you have to run every step of the way without benefit of a pit stop. And the long homestretch at Churchill Downs measures 1,234½ feet from the last turn to the finish line, quite a distance for a come-from-behind horse to get home first.

Except it doesn't always happen that way.

Usually, the race is over by the first minute and forty-eight seconds or so, the time it takes to run a mile and an eighth. The Derby certainly never lacks for drama or emotion (remember Alysheba's gallant effort in 1987 after stumbling in the upper stretch?), but when it comes to close shaves, the finishes are hardly ever decided by a whisker.

Generally speaking, if your horse is leading at the eighth pole, head for the mutuel windows. It's time to cash in all those tickets in your pocket.

Consider these numbers: Only five Derby winners in the last thirty years (1963 through 1992) took the lead in the final eighth of a mile. They were Proud Clarion in 1967, Foolish Pleasure in 1975, Alysheba in 1987, Strike the Gold in 1991, and Lil E. Tee in 1992—and all five of them were second with a furlong to go. Moreover, the last thrilling stretch-long battle was the 1969 renewal, won by Majestic Prince over Arts and Letters.

Whatever happened to the great Derby duels of Tomy Lee-Sword Dancer, Iron Liege-Gallant Man, Brokers Tip-Head Play, Ben Brush-Ben Eder? Where have you gone Carry Back, he of the breathtaking finish? Will the photo-finish camera ever be needed again on the first Saturday in May at Churchill Downs?

There hasn't been a nose finish in the Derby since Tomy Lee outbattled Sword Dancer in 1959. (A nose finish for first, that is. There have been two nose finishes between the next-to-last and last-place finishers in the past three decades—Verbatim edging Gleaming Sword in 1968 and Gold Stage nipping Hazard Duke in 1980. So much for trivia items.)

The lack of close finishes culminating a stretch battle seems to be more of a modern phenomenon in the Derby. The reason appears to trace to the size of the number of starters, the correlation being that the more horses in the race, the less chance for a tight finish. More on that later.

For now, let's put together an imaginary highlight film of the closest, most exciting finishes in the history of the Derby, which has been run continuously since 1875. It has to be imaginary because there is no film available for the very early Derbies. Not only that, but the photo-finish camera wasn't used at Churchill Downs until 1936, which brings us to an interesting question: Did all of the horses whose names appear on the Derby's honor roll of winners actually cross the wire first?

That Fighting Finish

You would have gotten an argument on who won the 1933 Derby from the late Herb Fisher, who rode Head Play. Fisher always swore that he actually won the race, but the placing judges thought otherwise, ruling that Brokers Tip triumphed.

This Derby was the famous Fighting Finish battle between Fisher and Don Meade, the jockey on Brokers Tip. Riding racehorses was a rougher business in those days than it is now. With no patrol film available in 1933 for stewards to use in scrutinizing races for infractions, jockeys were known to do anything short of homicide to win, whether it was leglocking other riders, slamming opponents into the rail, whipping other horses across the face or grabbing the bridles, reins, or saddlecloths of any moving object within reach.

The 1933 Derby's wild battle started after Charlie Corbett, who was riding a horse named Charley O., hollered to Fisher in the upper stretch: "Watch out for the inside!" Fisher glanced to the inside, and here came Brokers Tip slipping into contention. In an instantaneous decision that would leave him forever stamped as one of the Fighting Finish jockeys, Fisher guided Head Play, who was leading, over to the inside, closer and closer to the charging Brokers Tip. Before introductions could be made between the two horses, Meade thrust his hand out. "I actually was the one that grabbed him first," Meade recalled years later. "But I only grabbed him to protect myself. I thought he was going to shut me off or bump me real hard. That's why I put my hand out to keep him off. I wasn't going to have him put me through the fence."

Fisher, no Boy Scout in jockey silks, didn't guide Head Play over to the inside just to tell Meade the way home. "I went in to tighten things up on Meade," said Fisher. "I could have throwed him if I'da shut him off completely. If I'da completely cut him off and he'da had to stand up and pull up, well, hell, there'da been nuthin' to it. I'da won off two or three lengths. But I didn't want to shut him off completely. His horse's legs might have hit my horse's back legs and caused a fall. I didn't want to do that, so I just tightened it up."

And now the battle was on. "I pushed him off me to get

running room," said Meade, "and then he took ahold of me. Now I'm not going to sit there and let him lead me down there to the finish line. I couldn't push him away from me because he had ahold of me, so I had to get ahold of him. So from there down to the finish line, that's what it was—we grabbed, grabbed, grabbed all through the stretch. It was the survival of the fittest."

Once things got out of control, there was no calling off the rough stuff, even if the tug-of-war would take place down the homestretch in view of the stewards. This was the Derby, *the* Kentucky Derby, and each boy was determined to get the better of the other.

"When I put him in tight quarters," said Fisher, "he reached over and grabbed my saddlecloth at the eighth pole and held onto me. I tried to shake him loose by squeezing him against the fence, and he just held onto me. I was so amazed to think that he had the *nerve* to have ahold of me that I kinda lost my head, I blowed my top. I hit him across the head with my whip once or twice before the finish and then after the finish."

In a movie taken from high up at Churchill Downs and showing the last part of that Derby, Meade can be seen whipping Brokers Tip (that was *his* mount, remember) on the right side approaching the sixteenth pole. Meade didn't apply the whip again. Driving toward the wire, he held the reins snugly in his left hand and had the whip in his right hand. He reached over with his right hand to grab at his opponent. With about fifty yards to go, Fisher dropped his right hand, then recovered and pulled it back up, appearing to grab the mane of Head Play (nothing illegal there; that was *his* horse). Head Play appeared to hold a slight lead inside the sixteenth pole. Brokers Tip then seemed to edge in front, but in the last stride or two, Head Play made a final surge. Brokers Tip was declared the winner, triumphing by no more than two or three inches, according to *The Blood-Horse* magazine.

Two or three inches? A person watching the movie of the 1933 Derby can rerun the film time and time again in an effort to examine the race for details, but back then, the thirty to forty thousand fans—that's right, no more showed up in that Depression year—didn't have instant replays or slow-motion reruns. The stretch duel took place, and just like that, it was over.

After the horses whirled under the finish line in a flash, it was time for the placing judges to rule on who had won. How could anybody be certain as to who won such a close race? The verdict of the judges was that it was Brokers Tip. But did he actually beat Head Play? The movie of that 1933 Derby, though certainly not conclusive, could lead a skeptic to wonder whether it was Head Play who had won, a contention that Fisher made to his dying day in 1983.

As the two horses raced under the wire, there was no doubt in Meade's mind as to which one had won. "I know I did," he said.

Fisher, however, said, "I had taken the lead leaving the half-mile pole, so he had me to catch from there to home. I figured that I had just made it."

Fisher always regretted the fact that there was no photo-finish camera in those days. "I still think if they had had the photo-finish camera that they'da posted me as the winner, because I was on the outside and nowadays the photo-finish camera favors the outside horse," he said in 1974. "The judges in them days always favored the inside horse. Why I don't know, but they always did."

A Tough One to Call

If a photographer had been standing on the finish line at the 1889 Derby, he would have needed a wide-angle lens to catch all the action coming down the stretch. He also would have had to watch out that he didn't get run over by one of the contenders. There was Spokane on the rail and

Ben Brush, the 1896 Kentucky Derby winner. (Courtesy Keeneland Library, Lexington, Kentucky)

Carry Back, ridden by Johnny Sellers, came from far back to win the 1961 Kentucky Derby by three-quarters of a length over Crozier. (Courtesy Keeneland-Meadors)

Proctor Knott on the far outside. It seems that the favored Proctor Knott bolted at the top of the stretch and raced down the straightaway on the extreme outside.

With the width of the stretch separating the first two horses in an extremely close finish, the judges certainly had their work cut out in determining the outcome. They called it in Spokane's favor.

Ben Won . . . But Which One?

Through 1895, the Derby was run at a mile and a half. Then in 1896, the race was shortened to its current distance of a mile and a quarter.

Ben Brush and Ben Eder fought it out coming down the stretch in the '96 Derby, their riders using whip and spurs liberally. The finish was so close that some observers thought it was a dead heat. Quite a few in the crowd of fifteen thousand thought Ben Eder actually had won. Not so, said the judges. Ben Brush, ridden by Willie Simms, was ruled the winner. "Ah! it was a 'hoss-race!'" declared *The Thoroughbred Record* magazine. When the two Bens raced under the wire, "it was probably the only point in the last fifty yards at which a difference could be detected between the two horses," the magazine noted. "It is true there were many spectators who honestly believe that Ben Eder won, but the obstruction offered by the judges' box makes it impossible for anybody but the judges or those in the timers' stand to tell, and there seems no doubt, from the statements of those in these positions, that Simms (as a great jockey will) saved just one more effort in Ben Brush and using it in the last desperate leap, shot the hair on his nose in front of his shorter whiskered opponent."

However, John Taber (or Tabor), aboard Ben Eder, swore that his mount triumphed. "If ever a race was won, I won that one—and by a good head, too," he declared.

Move over, Herb Fisher. You've got company.

"Carry Back too far to make it . . . can't unless he hurries"

" . . . Carry Back is far out of it at this stage, and is moving is Carry Back. But they come into the stretch, it is still Globemaster, Four-and-Twenty, and Crozier ranges up on the outside, a three-horse battle. Carry Back too far to make it—can't unless he hurries."

No Derby winner ever faced a more challenging task turning for home than Carry Back did in 1961. He trailed the leader by more than thirteen lengths, which is some thirty-six yards. Here it was, a quarter of a mile to go in the Derby, and Carry Back had to make up approximately a third the length of a football field.

Could he possibly do it?

Bryan Field, announcing to a nationwide television audience, didn't give Carry Back much of a chance as the field came down the stretch in the 1961 Kentucky Derby. Sharp racing man that he was, Field should have known better than to ever count out this indomitable colt.

"I had lunch with Bryan Field that day," recalled Jack Price, the trainer and breeder of Carry Back. "He was drinking triple martinis, and I said, 'Bryan, there's fifteen horses in this field. It's tough enough to see them as it is.' He says, 'Oh, don't worry about me.'"

Okay, Bryan, okay. So you could handle things just fine in the Derby, but now there was a more important question: Could Carry Back? Many of his followers had given up hope. At this stage of the race, Price himself didn't think Carry Back would win.

A bit earlier in the race, Carry Back was even farther back going down the backstretch. Price had become worried and later admitted, "At the five-eighths pole, I thought he'd died. I didn't think we had any kind of a shot."

By midway on the turn, Carry Back had begun to do enough running to give Price renewed hope. "I thought we'd finish in the money." Down the stretch they charged, and the leaders were beginning to run out of gas. And here came Carry Back, ridden by Johnny Sellers. One by one Carry Back overtook his fading opponents. Crozier, meanwhile, made a move for the lead under jockey Braulio Baeza. "I'm passing Four-and-Twenty," Baeza recalled, "but I see this horse coming up on the outside. Can only be one. Carry Back."

"Crozier now on the outside in front. Crozier on the lead, and it looks for sure that Globemaster is beaten and so is Four-and-Twenty. And here comes Carry Back, the favorite."

Carry Back was fourth at the stretch call, trailing the front-running Crozier by a full four and a half lengths. With just thirteen or so seconds left in the race, Carry Back still was some thirty-eight feet off the lead. That was almost thirteen yards that he needed to make up. Could he do it? Time was running out.

Price had predicted that the Derby would be strictly a two-horse affair: Carry Back versus Crozier. The confident Price also said that he believed Carry Back would get the best of Crozier again. "We have beaten Crozier three times, and we can do it again," Price declared.

Inside the eighth pole, Carry Back surged to third—and then second. Now only Crozier was left to be caught, but just a few seconds remained. Price himself didn't think his pride and joy would make it. "I was going to be satisfied with second money of twenty-five thousand dollars to make expenses," he said afterward. "I'm no hog."

"Carry Back after Crozier. Crozier with a chance to turn the tables, Carry Back charging, Carry Back coming. CARRY BACK IN FRONT. CARRY BACK'S GONNA WIN. HERE'S THE FINISH—CARRY BACK BY THREE-QUARTERS, Crozier is second . . ."

Carry Back had made up more lengths in the home-stretch than any Derby winner in history. What to do for an encore? Well, just two weeks later in Baltimore, he came through with still another powerful finishing kick to win the Preakness. He was second at the stretch call, four lengths behind Globemaster, and appeared hopelessly beaten. Yet, he unleashed a furious surge at the end to win again by three-quarters of a length.

The Shoe Lost One, Then Won One

The Derbies from 1953 through 1959 should have been dubbed "Close Encounters of the Churchill Downs Kind." Less than four and a half lengths determined the outcome of those seven races.

The Derby had gone since the Fighting Finish Derby without a nose verdict, but then it had two in three years. Bill Shoemaker lost one of those decisions, then came back to win the other. Both horses he rode—Gallant Man and Tomy Lee—were owned by people from Midland, Texas.

Ralph Lowe, who owned Gallant Man, had a dream during Derby Week of 1957 that his colt was charging down the stretch in the big race, on his way to certain victory, when his rider suddenly misjudged the finish line and pulled up prematurely, costing him the race.

Shoemaker, who was informed of the dream, then went out and did just that. Iron Liege held the lead in the upper stretch, but Gallant Man was gaining ground. Down the stretch they rolled, Iron Liege on the rail and Gallant Man coming on, a two-horse battle that had the crowd cheering wildly. Up in a clubhouse box, Johnny Nerud, the trainer of Gallant Man, punched Lowe on the back and said, "Go down to the winner's circle and get your roses and take 'em back to Texas."

Then, as the horses passed the sixteenth pole, something incredible happened. Exactly as Lowe had dreamed, his jockey stood up on Gallant Man. It happened so fast that only a few people noticed it. In a flash, Shoemaker was back in his saddle and riding again, but in the closing yards the luckless Gallant Man couldn't overhaul Iron Liege, who won by a nose.

In 1959, a crowd of 72,951 turned out in ninety-four-degree weather at Churchill Downs, the hottest Derby Day in history, and what they were treated to was the hottest stretch battle in the race's history. The noise was deafening as the field swung into the stretch, particularly when thousands of women started screaming and shouting after the track announcer called out that Silver Spoon, a filly, was racing in third place and looking good.

Looking even better were Tomy Lee and Sword Dancer, the two front-running horses. At the same time that the women were shrieking, another yell went up, but the only person who could hear it was Bill Boland, who was moving Sword Dancer past Tomy Lee and into the lead near the quarter pole. At that point, Shoemaker, thinking that Tomy Lee was finished and wouldn't be able to regain the lead, called out to Boland: "Good luck—go on and get it."

To Shoemaker's surprise, just when he thought Sword Dancer was about to pull away, Tomy Lee dug in and came back. With the crowd yelling itself hoarse, Sword Dancer and Tomy Lee hooked up in a dramatic stretch duel, one that was marked by sharp contact between the battling horses. Passing the three-sixteenths pole, Tomy Lee came out into Sword Dancer, who held a slight lead. Then, near the eighth pole, Sword Dancer slammed in against Tomy Lee. Through the final furlong, there was continued contact between the two horses, and with fifty yards to go Sword Dancer, still holding the lead, looked as if he was going to hang on. But this time Shoemaker knew where the finish line was—and he knew he still had time to get there. In a brilliant display of riding, he called on Tomy Lee for just one final surge, and the colt charged back to win in a photo finish—by a nose. Boland promptly claimed a foul against Tomy Lee. The stewards studied the patrol film, and seventeen or eighteen minutes after the race, they reached a decision. The foul claim was disallowed, and Tomy Lee, owned by Mr. and Mrs. Fred W. Turner Jr., was the winner.

Shoemaker was certain that the bump that Tomy Lee received at the eighth pole actually won the race for him. "It made Tomy Lee change his lead," Shoemaker explained, referring to the fact that horses lead with one of their forelegs while they're running. "He was on his left lead all the way from the backstretch to the three-eighths pole, and into the stretch he was still on his left lead, where a horse normally will change his lead. Then when Sword Dancer bumped him, it hit him hard enough that it made him switch to his right lead, and that gave him enough energy to come on again and beat him. If Sword Dancer had let him alone, Tomy Lee never would have changed leads and never would have won either."

Lost—and Won—in the Fifties

The Fifties produced other eventful stretch runs. In 1956, Needles dropped far back in the early going, more than twenty-three lengths off the lead. Then as the colt passed the five-eighths pole in next-to-last place, jockey Dave Erb's world collapsed momentarily—Needles had let go of the bit. "I thought, 'Migawd, what's gonna happen now?'" Erb would later say. "But he took hold again, and we were all right."

Not really. Needles still had to wend past fifteen opponents. When the skillful Erb gave him the word, Needles took off like a bullet and somehow avoided any traffic problems as he swept to seventh or eighth place at the top of the stretch. He shot to second at midstretch, caught

Fabius at the sixteenth pole, and went on to win by three-quarters of a length in an amazing finish.

In 1953, Native Dancer was no more than two and a half lengths off the lead near the head of the homestretch, and midway down the straightaway trailed by just a length and a half. Native Dancer had dead aim on the leader, Dark Star. All he had to do was pass him. But he couldn't. Dark Star won in a stirring finish, holding on to edge Native Dancer by a head. That loss would be the only blemish in twenty-two career starts for Native Dancer . . . but his descendants would get even for him on the first Saturday in May at Churchill Downs.

A Full Century of Close Finishes

In the 1960s, three of the closest four finishes of the decade were won by horses who carried the blood of Native Dancer. In 1964, Northern Dancer, a grandson of Native Dancer, held off Hill Rise by a neck in a pulsating battle. Two years later, Kauai King, a son of Native Dancer, prevailed by a half-length. And in 1969, Majestic Prince, another grandson of Native Dancer, outdueled Arts and Letters by a neck, with Dike just a half-length back in third.

No highlight film of close Derby finishes would be complete without Bold Venture's head decision over Brevity in 1936 . . . Jet Pilot's victory—also by a head—over Phalanx, who edged Faultless by that same margin for second, in 1947 . . . Azra's nose verdict over Huron in 1892 . . . Plaudit's flying finish that produced a close win over the favored Lieber Karl in 1898 . . . Alan-a-Dale's narrow triumph over Inventor in 1902. And, in 1965, Dapper Dan's backers were trying all the Body English that they could possibly muster to get him home at the end, but this stretch runner, who made up four lengths in the final furlong, lost by a neck to Lucky Debonair.

Since the Majestic Prince-Arts and Letters battle in 1969, the Derby hasn't had the first two finishers fight it out the length of the stretch in a nip-and-tuck battle. Interestingly, the 1969 Derby drew only eight starters. In the 1970s, the Derby fields averaged 14.9 starters, and in the 1980s they averaged 17.1.

That's not to say that the Derby hasn't had some exciting finishes since 1969. In 1976, Bold Forbes led by a half-length over Honest Pleasure in the stretch until moving away near the end to win by a length. Woodchopper, trapped in a cumbersome field in the upper stretch, finally shook loose and was flying in the closing yards of the 1981 Derby. He fell three-quarters of a length short in his bid to catch Pleasant Colony. In 1988, Forty Niner made a furious finish himself. In third place, four lengths off the lead at the stretch call, Forty Niner was charging at the end but was unable to overtake the determined Winning Colors, who won by a neck.

The Breeders' Cup Classic, run at the same mile-and-a-quarter distance as the Derby, has drawn just ninety-five starters in its nine-year history (1984–92) and has been decided by a total of six and a half lengths. During that time, the Derby has attracted all of 147 starters, and the total winning margins in the eight races have been twenty-one lengths.

West Coast trainer Charlie Whittingham has won both races twice—Ferdinand capturing the 1986 Derby by two and a quarter lengths and the 1987 Classic by a nose, and Sunday Silence triumphing by two and a half lengths in the 1989 Derby and by a neck in the 1989 Classic.

With the Derby permitting as many as twenty starters, those big fields can lead to traffic problems, which means that contenders sometimes encounter all kinds of trouble. "A lot of horses that run in the Derby don't belong," Whittingham said. "By the time you get to the Breeders' Cup, you've eliminated most of the ones that don't belong, and the Breeders' Cup horses are all the best of the bunch, so you've got a little more competition."

Said retired Kentucky state steward Keene Daingerfield: "In any type of race, a horse that gets loose on the lead is hard to beat. This is especially true in large fields, in which the others have decisions to make which may be the wrong ones and, in any case, must pass a lot of horses, some of them staggering. Then, too, contenders may get off badly and anticipated early contention doesn't materialize. To win the Derby, you almost have to have your horse in contention with half a mile to go. If I had a Derby horse, I'd want him there or thereabouts, all the way."

Mike Barry, the late Louisville newspaperman who saw all but four Derbies from 1922 through 1991, said in a 1990 interview: "It's always a thrill to see a horse win the Derby, but we've had very few real horse races in the last twenty, thirty years. I think having twenty horses certainly makes racing luck a bigger factor than it ought to be, because with twenty horses, the jockeys can't ride the kind of race they want. They're always using their horses to get a position to get out of the traffic. I think that affects the race. I like the fourteen-horse limit that Pimlico has for the Preakness. I don't know why they can't have a fourteen-horse limit for the Derby."

Col. M. Lewis Clark, founder of the Kentucky Derby. (Courtesy Keeneland Library, Lexington, Kentucky)

3

The Derby's Founding Father, Colonel Clark

WANTED: Enterprising young man willing to serve in dual role as racetrack executive and presiding judge. No financial security. Must be willing to serve without pay—and even pay racetrack bills out of his own pocket. This person must always strive to uphold the rules of racing, even if it means risking his life. No experience needed.

M. Lewis Clark Jr. didn't apply for that job at Churchill Downs back in the nineteenth century, because, of course, no such advertisement ever appeared in the newspapers. However, a job of that kind did exist, and, as it turned out, Clark was the perfect man for it.

He was the founder of the Downs and the Kentucky Derby, the man responsible for launching this event on the road to its current status of America's most celebrated horse race.

At the time of the Derby's inception, Clark envisioned great things for the race, but little did he know what the future held in store for him. Always with the good of Churchill Downs in mind, Clark would go the next two decades without receiving pay during certain financially troublesome times for the track. He would even open his own wallet to help pay track bills. Moreover, he was so obsessed with following the rules of racing that he repeatedly made many horsemen angry and, once, was even shot by a disgruntled owner against whom Clark had taken action.

Since the inaugural Churchill Downs meeting in the spring of 1875, the track has held a race in honor of its founding father—first called the Clark Stakes and later the Clark Handicap.

It's only appropriate that this race is named after a man of Clark's stature.

Clark, a brilliant racetrack president and presiding judge, was an ingenious individual, a man who was far ahead of his time. When Lynn Stone was named Churchill Downs president in December 1969, it was reported that he, at forty-four, was the youngest man ever to assume that position. The report was in error by a full fifteen years.

Clark was just twenty-nine years old when he opened the doors at Churchill Downs on May 17, 1875, the day of the first Kentucky Derby. Attention was focused throughout the country on whether Clark's new track would be successful.

The Civil War had been over for ten years, but the South was still feeling the effects of the destruction that the fighting and plundering had wrought on its horse centers. Near the end of the war and for some time afterward, guerrilla bands in Federal uniforms raided farms and seized valuable horses.

Kentucky's horse industry had been hurt, but not as badly as many other states. Still, even though racing was conducted at the Kentucky Association course in Lexington, breeders were distressed because Louisville was without a track. Racing had been held previously in Louisville, as early as 1783 on a downtown street, but it always had been an unsuccessful enterprise, the last venture resulting in the bankruptcy of the Woodlawn Course in 1870.

Then in 1872 a group of breeders, some on the verge of

abandoning their operations, asked Clark, a Louisville socialite, if he could do anything to resurrect the sport in Louisville.

Clark agreed to help the breeders. It was first intended that a new track would be established at once, but that plan was delayed. Instead of rushing into action, as others might have, Clark went to Europe and carefully studied racing in England and France. Thus, Meriwether Lewis Clark Jr., a grandson of William Clark of the famous Lewis and Clark expedition, set out for Europe on a scouting mission of his own.

Since Clark had no background in racetrack management, having worked in the banking and tobacco businesses, the trip to Europe was a genuine learning experience for him. In England, Clark was deeply impressed with the interest generated by a series of tradition-rich stakes races—the Epsom Derby (a race named for the twelfth Earl of Derby), the Epsom Oaks, the St. Leger Stakes, and the Ascot Gold Cup. In France, Clark studied the country's wagering methods.

After spending two years or so learning the ways of European racing, Clark returned to Louisville and summoned the breeders to a meeting. He told them of his plan for the establishment of a racetrack in Louisville. He outlined the formation of a permanent series of races modeled after the English classics. He envisioned a race called the Kentucky Derby, which would be patterned after the Epsom Derby. At the very outset, Clark forecast greatness for the Kentucky Derby, predicting that in a decade the winner of the race would be worth more or sell for more than the farm on which he was bred and raised.

Clark enthusiastically went to work. In 1874, he formed a corporation formally known as the Louisville Jockey Club and Driving Park Association. He raised thirty-two thousand dollars in capital and selected a track site that was just a few miles south of the heart of the city. A primary reason for the choice of this property was that instead of buying it, Clark could lease it from his two uncles, John and Henry Churchill. After the land was cleared and the one-mile racing strip graded and constructed, the funds were exhausted. And still there was no grandstand. Coming to the rescue of Clark's group was W. H. Thomas, a prominent Louisville merchant who loaned the track enough money to build a small, wooden grandstand.

Unfavorable winter weather, combined with a shortage of labor and building materials, delayed construction of the grandstand, and the work was completed just in time for the opening day of the 1875 spring meeting, the day that Aristides won the inaugural Kentucky Derby. Although just a young man, Clark handled the first Derby like an old pro. No major problems arose during the day, although once some spectators did complain loudly because of a delay at the start of a race. But they were silenced at once by the decisive Clark, who demonstrated from the start that he was a forceful track president, not a figurehead.

Clark, who became known as a colonel in the finest Kentucky tradition, used good, old-fashioned horse sense in running the racetrack. For example, he did all he could to attract the fair sex to the track. He reasoned that if the ladies enjoyed themselves at the races, it would naturally follow that they would encourage their husbands' participation in this pastime.

A logical thinker, Clark.

The author of many turf rules, Clark commanded high pay for his services as a racing judge. At Garfield Park in Chicago, he once had a contract that covered pay of a hundred dollars a day, a personal servant in the judges' stand, a carriage to transport him to and from the track, and his living expenses. The tall, massive Clark always stood majestically in the judges' stand, flawlessly dressed, a flower in his buttonhole and binoculars to his eyes.

Clark was a perfectionist and a highly sensitive man who, it was once said, "often exaggerated a small matter arising in the course of his turf business until it seemed to him to be a reflection upon his integrity." And he was a man of the highest integrity.

In 1897, *The Thoroughbred Record* reported that Clark had set down jockey Bozeman after a race in Chicago. The dispatch said Clark "will notify Owner L.H. Ezell to remove his horses. Ezell had Pepper in the fifth race, with his jockey, Bozeman, up. The race, a mile and a quarter, looked like a 'cinch' for Ezell's horse, and he went to the post a 7 to 20 favorite, but the best it could do was to finish third. The judges did not fancy the manner in which Bozeman rode and declared all bets off. Sharp eyes and a tab has been kept on Bozeman and the in-and-out manner in which Ezell's horses had been racing, hence, the above rulings."

Clark never would have won a popularity contest among horsemen, but that was not his ambition. His aim was honest racing—and, if his strict enforcement of the rules angered horsemen, so be it. Yet he always commanded respect.

An anonymous horseman once was quoted: "I do not like a bone in Col. Clark's body, but he is the straightest turfman in the world and is recognized as such all over the world. If I had to race for my life I would rather have Col. Clark . . . get in the judges' stand than any other man I know of."

Clark's reputation also was mentioned in a *Turf, Field and Farm* article that stated: "His rulings, while just, have not at all times suited a certain class of turf speculators, but they are fearlessly and honestly made and intended for the good of the public. He is a law unto himself and does not permit technical quibbles to blind his sense of justice. He can smell a turf job as far as a buzzard scents carrion, and he has a faculty of nipping disreputable schemes in the bud. Of remarkable courage, devoid of prejudice and absolutely impartial, he is a man whom no rascal can outwit and no bullying daunt."

In a story after his death, *The Thoroughbred Record* stated, "Years ago, when Col. Clark first became President of the old Louisville Jockey Club, he established a reputation as a most dangerous man to be trifled with. Owner after owner and jockey upon jockey has come under the iron rule of the famous originator of the first Western Turf Congress, and to Jockey Hogan, whose suspicious ride on Laura May . . . belongs the distinction of being the last to suffer for palpable and undisputed crookedness in the saddle from the hands of the deceased turf judge."

Clark's dedication to honest racing was illustrated before the celebrated four-mile match race between Ten Broeck and Mollie McCarthy on July 4, 1878, at the Louisville Jockey Club. (The track's name hadn't yet been changed to Churchill Downs.) Clark heard of a possible fix in the works, the suspicions arising that Harry Colston, the trainer of Ten Broeck, and jockey, William Walker, would throw the race.

Clark took precautions to assure, as best he could, that the race would be run on the level. He sent police to watch Ten Broeck's barn. Special security was provided at Mollie McCarthy's stable, too, and the feed for both horses was locked up. Clark made it a point to drop by Ten Broeck's barn himself every morning, inquiring about the horse and asking how fast he had exercised. Clark also told the Ten Broeck camp how fast he thought each mile should be run.

Moreover, Clark made no secret of what would happen to Walker if the race wasn't run on the up and up.

"I hear there are suspicions that you are going to throw this race," Clark told Walker. "You will be watched the whole way, and if you do not ride to win, a rope will be put about your neck and you will be hung to that tree yonder

(Clark pointed to a tree just across from the judges' stand) *and I will help to do it."*

Walker attempted to say that, under the circumstances, he didn't want to ride in the race, but Clark wouldn't allow him to speak. The race turned out to be a farce. Mollie McCarthy conked out, not even finishing the race, and Ten Broeck won in extremely slow time. Despite all the safeguards taken by Clark, some suspected that Ten Broeck had been drugged anyway.

For nearly two hours after the race, Clark was unconscious, the victim of a sunstroke. That's probably not all he suffered from that day. It's a good bet he received a king-sized headache trying to uphold the integrity of the race. As *The Spirit of the Times* noted, Clark "pledged his word to protect the public; declared he would throw the mantle of the Jockey Club over both horses, and that it should be a fair race; that the public should not be swindled. His persistent energy and continued asseverations appeased, in a measure, the fears of the public, but we fear that the reaction upon him and his club may be so great that he may rue the active part in the matter he has been induced to take. He put a police over both horses, yet, in spite of all his precautions and active watchfulness, the Kentuckians 'do say' that Ten Broeck got that much-dreaded and long-talked-of 'cup of cold pizen,' or he would have done better."

Clark knew all too well that enforcing rules could be risky business. More than once his life was endangered because of his rulings. A notable incident occurred in 1879. It seems that Clark refused to allow Capt. T. G. Moore, a well-known horseman from Crab Orchard, Kentucky, to start his horses in a stakes race because he hadn't made certain payments. Clark and Moore exchanged some harsh words at the track.

Moore, it seems, had the idea that Clark was deliberately trying to insult him. Witnesses heard Moore speak

disparagingly of Clark, saying such things as, "He's a God-
damn liar. He did mean to insult me." One witness said
that he didn't think Clark heard that expression by Moore.
"The next I saw of the affair Capt. Moore and Col. Clark
were standing between the grandstand and the clubroom,"
the witness said. "Col. Clark was laughing and had his
hand upon Capt. Moore's hand, which led me to believe
the difficulty had been settled."

But it hadn't.

Their paths were to cross later that evening at the Galt
House, the grand hotel located at First and Main. Clark,
who had been warned about Moore, obtained a pistol from
a Galt House employee before Moore arrived at the hotel
with his son, George. The elder Moore, who apparently
had been drinking, and Clark proceeded to have a discus-
sion in the hotel's rotunda before they entered a private
office. Moore demanded a public apology, saying that
Clark had insulted him.

"I replied that no insult was intended and hoped that he
was satisfied," Clark later testified. "He said, 'No, by God, I
ain't! You've insulted me publicly, by God, and you have
got to make a public apology.' I replied, 'You'll wait a long
while to get it.' We were seated at a desk. He got up and
said, 'Then you can take the consequences.' Believing he
was going to strike me, I hit him with my fist between the
eyes and knocked him toward the door, or rather against
it. He then put one of his hands—I think his left hand, but
am not positive—toward his side or back, and I drew my
pistol and covered him and said, 'Two can play at that
game.' He said something, and I said, 'Get out of here!' He
rushed out of the door . . . and (I) heard him hallooing
something and saw two men, as I shut the door, standing
just outside of it. It was a ground-glass, paneled door. I
stepped to the door, caught hold of the knob and put my
foot against the door. Was looking around at the same time

to see if I could get my pistol, but couldn't reach it. I heard the glass crash, and I was shot."

When hit, Clark was heard to yell, "I'm killed!" The wound turned out to be ugly and painful, but not dangerous. The ball entered Clark's right side, near the breastbone, and lodged under the muscles of the right arm.

Moore's account of the incident differed from Clark's. In an incomplete interview with a newsman, Moore said that when he entered the Galt House he was accosted by Clark. Moore said Clark "drew a pistol and called me a son of a bitch." Moore said that he was unarmed and that Clark "knew at the time that I was unarmed, and . . ." That's all Moore said in the interview because, just then, his attorney entered the room and told his client not to say another word. So much for getting both sides of a story.

Later Moore's son, George, testified that Clark threatened to shoot his father if he didn't get out of the office.

John Connor, night watchman at the Galt House, offered this testimony: "Was in the rotunda about half past 8 o'clock, when I heard a quarrel between Col. Clark and Capt. Moore in the private office. I first heard the difficulty when I was turning out the gas at the telegraph office. I walked slowly toward the private office and saw Capt. Moore standing in the doorway, the door being wide open. Col. Clark was standing about four feet back in the office. The first thing I heard was Capt. Moore saying, 'Give me my pistol.' Col. Clark said, 'Don't give him any weapon.' I stepped forward and, catching hold of Capt. Moore, asked him to be quiet. He immediately pointed a pistol at my head and said, 'Damn you, get out of my way or I'll shoot you.' I ducked my head and ran into the water-closet."

Moore was ruled off the track by the Executive Committee of the Louisville Jockey Club because of his language and conduct on the track during the meeting. He was reinstated the following year. Clark himself wrote to the Executive Committee, asking for Moore's reinstatement. "On account of the condition of the family of T. G. Moore, caused by the action of your committee in retiring him from the turf and from assurances of apology and regret for his conduct, I desire to have justice tempered with mercy, and request that you will restore him to the privileges of the turf," Clark wrote.

Another incident, this one with controversial horseman Ed Corrigan, revealed Clark's bold nature. "It was at the meeting of the Turf Congress at Cincinnati, that Turfman Corrigan bobbed up with a wordy attack on Col. Clark for upholding the claims of the Harlem track to official sanction," *The Courier-Journal* reported. "The latter was quick to resent. Col. Clark covered his opponent with a gun and made him back down in complete style."

Unlike certain track executives who for one reason or another are reluctant publicly to make predictions on races, Clark wasn't bashful about saying who he thought would win the Derby. As a judge, of course, Clark never wagered money on races, but he was known to bet a new hat on the outcome of the Derby.

And after a race, Clark would speak his mind openly.

Clark came right out after the 1889 Derby and said that the narrowly beaten runner-up, Proctor Knott, who bolted at the top of the stretch and raced down the straightaway on the extreme outside, would have defeated Spokane if he had been ridden by a stronger jockey. Pike Barnes, who rode Proctor Knott, said the same thing. "It's all my fault," Barnes said. "I ain't big enough for him. That's the greatest 3-year-old in the world, and if I could have held him he would have won that race hands down."

Following the 1898 Derby, Clark referred to the victorious Plaudit, ridden by Willie Simms, as "a great colt," but he added, "I think it was the extra five pounds and the condition of the track that beat Lieber Karl (the runner-up). It was as fair a race in every way as I ever saw, and Simms displayed excellent horsemanship. Live weight against dead weight also militated against Lieber Karl."

Clark wasn't afraid to speak out, even if it meant sometimes irritating certain gentlemen of the Fourth Estate. For example, Clark believed it would be desirable for turf writers to refrain from betting. It was his opinion that betting by writers influenced their objectivity in reporting.

A Louisville racing reporter took issue with Clark, writing: "A man who allows his eyesight, his utterances, or his writing to be influenced by a bet is not fit to be turf editor of a reputable newspaper and could not be one long." (If only this old-time scribe could see some of the wild-eyed, two-fisted, overly opinionated bettors in press boxes today, he might wonder if Clark wasn't right after all.)

Despite his objection to betting by the working press, Clark certainly was no enemy of the writers. Quite to the contrary. He would invite newsmen to the clubhouse for champagne, and he'd praise them for accurate reporting. He had a certain charm and charisma that made good copy for writers. Newspapers documented his every move on Derby Day. An 1887 *Louisville Commercial* advance story on the Derby stated that Clark would be at the race "wearing a new spring suit, and showing up ruddy and happy in the Judges' stand with a flower in his button-hole."

In 1884, *The Courier-Journal* provided the following account of Clark's trip to the track on Derby Day: "President Clark was the first to start from the Pendennis on the big red vehicle belonging to the Jockey Club. He drove four large bays. As he drove through town he plucked a flower here and there and when he reached the grounds the usual 'bouquet of beautiful rose-buds' was on the coach."

Fifty years after his death society editor Marion Green of *The Louisville Times* wrote that in the old days "Clark could be seen driving out to the track in his tallyho. Every day during the race meet, Clark would start out from the Pendennis Club with his coach filled with pretty girls in frilled organdies, holding fluffy parasols over their heads to guard their lily-white skins from the outrageous rays of the spring sunshine."

Everything at the Downs seemed to center around Clark. Even the weather. It was a favorite expression to predict "Clark weather"—that is, fair, sunny weather—on Derby Day. "Clark luck" was said to account for such favorable weather. And the day of the Clark Stakes was known as "Clark Day."

It was said that no man in Louisville was more widely known than Clark.

A man with a taste for sparkling champagne, Clark liked to throw parties and dinners. He was a big spender—and a big man, too, weighing as much as three hundred pounds. Clark frequented the best nightclubs in cities he visited, and in Louisville he entertained with great lavishness at the Pendennis Club and at the track's clubhouse, which also served as his residence at times.

Clark took pride in his dinner decorations and arrangements. His Derby dinners at the Pendennis Club had everything and were the talk of the town.

Those who attended his dinner following the 1889 Derby never forgot the extravagance of it all. The interior of a table was laid out with sand and gravel in the form of a miniature Churchill Downs. Small wooden horses and jockeys were arranged on the track to represent their order of finish in the Derby. Horse talk, of course, was the chief topic of conversation, and by the end of the dinner every lady in attendance knew virtually by heart how the race had been run and the margin of finish between each of the horses. At another of Clark's Derby dinners, the inside of a circular table arrangement was decorated with the reproduction of a peaceful country pond. A miniature fountain sprayed playfully from the center of a tank, which was covered by moss and ferns. Newly hatched goslings swam about in the pond, greedily eating crumbs flipped in the water by Clark's amused guests.

A special visitor to an early Derby was Helena Modjeska, the famous Polish actress, who was accompanied by her husband, Count Bozenta Chlapowski. Clark had a Derby Day breakfast at the clubhouse for the count and countess, along with a few exclusive guests. For the occasion Clark prepared a mint julep, filling a huge silver bowl that he intended to be shared as a loving cup among his guests.

"It is for you first of all, Madame," Clark told the beautiful actress. "We drink to the greatest race of all times, the Kentucky Derby."

The countess took a sip, and then, instead of passing the cup along, she kept the drink and exclaimed, "My dear, Colonel Clark! Eet ees supreme! Won't you please feex anodder such dreenk for ze Count?"

Clark promptly went about the business of producing enough mint juleps for all his guests.

For all the fun that Clark had running the Derby, he eventually would suffer financial failure. The track simply was not a sound business venture. Clark did all he could to keep the track going. In a spirit that few (if any) modern-day executives would emulate, he was known to pay track bills from his personal account. According to one news account, Clark spent thirty-eight hundred dollars out of his pocket to cover the loss incurred at the 1893 fall meeting. Another story said that during the 1894 spring meeting, the track lost some eight thousand dollars, money for which Clark principally assumed the responsibility. Not only that, but Clark hadn't drawn back salary of eleven thousand dollars.

George B. "Brownie" Leach, the late public relations director at Churchill Downs and racing historian, once recalled a story stating that for a number of years early in the track's history Clark dipped into his own pocket to help pay the bills. "In the first half of the 1880s, the track made money for the first time since it was started," Leach said, "and all bills owed by Churchill Downs were paid—except Col. Clark had never received a dime for anything he ever did or spent on the racetrack. He carried the thing. That's what he did. He was determined to run a high-class racetrack. I think that he was as outstanding a racetrack operator as anybody I ever read about or heard about."

Finally, after the 1894 spring meeting, the Clark regime ended, and Churchill Downs was sold. Clark was retained as presiding judge under the new management, a position he held until his death.

Clark was normally a jovial, affable sort, but his personality changed in the latter period of his life. When he arrived at Memphis in the spring of 1899 to serve as presiding judge at the Montgomery Park meeting, friends couldn't help but notice that he was particularly despondent. The death of a close friend, James Richardson, seemed to trouble him, and he often mentioned that all of the old gang to which he once belonged was passing away.

Although never seriously ill, he had been bothered for some years with rheumatism and occasional attacks of gout. He also had liver trouble. But now bad health was getting the best of him. According to one report, his physician said Clark was suffering from melancholia; according to another it was neurasthenia. Unable to stand the demands of his duties at the track, Clark frequently complained of fatigue. He had trouble staying awake, except at the track. At the theater or the hotel, or during business transactions or even while engaging in conversation, he would suddenly doze off—and only with difficulty could he be aroused. This condition was attributed to his extreme obesity.

His health became bad enough that he was forced to remain in his hotel and miss the races one day at the 1899 Montgomery Park meeting. He never was to see another race. The next morning he took his own life in his hotel room. His body was found lying across his bed with a revolver clutched tightly in his right hand. "Death must have been instantaneous," it was reported. "The bullet entered the right side of the head, about two inches in front of the temple, and ranged downward into the brain."

Clark left no message explaining his suicide. His health was believed to be the reason for the act. Financial difficulty also was mentioned as a possible motive. But Charles F. Price, an intimate friend and associate of Clark, insisted that as far as he could determine, Clark's financial condition was as sound as it had been in years.

"Only a short while ago, to my personal knowledge, he held securities amounting to nearly $40,000," Price said. "Col. Clark always had a fear that as he grew older, he would be incapacitated for active work. His feeling on this subject was so strong that time after time I have seen him in the stand when he much better should have been in bed. For three days before his death he had to be helped from his bed to his carriage, and the day before his death was the first day in over a quarter of a century that sickness had prevented his appearance in the stand. . . . I have no doubt that ill health alone was responsible for his death."

C. W. Dudley, a Lexington, Kentucky, man, said that just one week before the suicide he had dined with Clark at the Peabody cafe in Memphis. "He was decidedly blue," Dudley said. "For some time he had suffered with gout, and last week he stumbled and fell while crossing the street. He was certainly not financially embarrassed, for his income reached something like $10,000 or $12,000 a year."

Clark, whose remains were buried in Louisville's Cave Hill Cemetery, was survived by his wife, a son, and two daughters.

Price paid Clark a fitting final tribute.

"For over a quarter of a century Col. Clark had been identified with the highest and best interests of the turf, and the world of honest sport can spare almost any man better than he. Fearless, impartial and incorruptible, from the day he first stepped into a judge's stand until the pathetic ending of his life, he made a brave fight for honest racing, challenging even the admiration of the rascals whom he had been instrumental in outlawing."

4

Col. Matt Winn—Mr. Derby

A fabulous character in every respect was the man who was christened Martin Joseph Winn but became Matt Winn. He could give cards and spades to Barnum and beat him. The Kentucky Derby is a monument to him. It's his baby and his alone. He will always be a part of it, even more a part of it than the spired towers at Churchill Downs. He alone made it what it is today.

Arthur Daley
The New York Times
1949

The Kentucky Derby, long recognized as America's most popular and most ballyhooed horse race, owes its very survival to this one man, Col. Matt Winn.

Putting almost a half-century of his life into making the Derby a happening, he left all of us his legacy that we celebrate every year on the first Saturday in May at Churchill Downs.

Winn had spirit and style. He liked horses, and he liked people. He was as much at ease conversing with a millionaire as he was talking with the little guy. And he knew plenty of millionaires.

"Colonel Winn's personality enabled him to walk with the titans," the late Downs public relations director George B.

Col. Matt Winn . . . Mr. Derby. (Courtesy Churchill Downs Inc./Kinetic Corp.)

"Brownie" Leach wrote in *The Blood-Horse* magazine. "He numbered among his close friends outstanding men in finance, industry, politics, commerce, and the professions. It was obvious they enjoyed his company and respected his judgment.

"Probably through sheer personality he first persuaded the country's most prominent stables to nominate horses and run them in the Kentucky Derby. . . . The same magnetic personality drew the country's leading writers, both in and out of sports. Articles by Damon Runyon, Grantland Rice, Irvin S. Cobb, and countless others provide records of that attraction. . . . His belief in the importance of New York to the Derby accounted for his making that city his headquarters during most of his 'off season.' If his evenings there were not occupied by social engagements, he likely would be in a night spot with writers or have them visiting his apartment in the Waldorf Towers."

Leach once told this writer: "I've never worked for any man like him. When I knew him intimately, he was in his eighties, and there was no question that he mellowed a lot. He was an awful nice, wonderful, elderly man who was just as sharp as he could be. Before that, by his own accounts, he was tougher than pig iron. What I admired most in Winn was his extreme loyalty to the people that worked for him."

A fixture at Churchill Downs, Winn served as track president from 1938 to 1949. But make no mistake about who was in charge almost from the beginning of Winn's employment at the Downs in 1902. Winn was always calling the shots in those earlier years while certain other men serving as Churchill Downs' president were nothing more than figureheads.

As Leach put it, "Winn was the boss. He ran the thing from the time that he came in there."

The late Stanley Hugenberg, long associated with Churchill Downs, said Winn was one of a kind. "He could turn a smile on like you turn a faucet," said Hugenberg. "He had access to a lot of people. He was worldwide. I've seen some damn smart people and some damn rich people, but in my judgment Colonel Winn was the only man I saw that could have done what he did with the Derby. He took it from just an ordinary race and made it worldwide, possibly the best-known race in the world."

A great asset of Winn's was his ability to charm the press. Winn realized the benefit of the New York media. "Give me the five best writers in New York on my side, and you can have the rest," he said.

Winn would go to New York and check in at the Waldorf, and big-name writers such as Grantland Rice, Damon Runyon, and Bill Corum would flock to his room. As one old-timer recalled, "They all knew Winn was good copy—and good company!"

He ran up exorbitant entertainment expenses with the news media. "The writers fell in love with Winn, to whom they always could turn for a fresh quote or a free drink," Billy Reed once wrote in *The Courier-Journal*. "He never let anyone pick up a check, especially a reporter."

Certain out-of-town writers formerly had travel and/or room expenses paid by the Downs. "That went on for quite a long time," recalled retired sports editor Earl Ruby of *The Courier-Journal*. "I think most racetracks were doing it."

Nothing stopped Winn in his goal to establish the Derby as a great race. Not reformers, not the Great Depression, not two world wars.

To fully appreciate Winn's devotion to the Derby, the clock needs to be turned back to 1902, back when the race was anything but the glamorous spectacle that it is today.

In the latter part of the 1800s and the early years of this century, the Derby was in a slump. Churchill Downs was having financial difficulties, and the outlook was so bleak following the 1902 Derby that it appeared the track would be permanently closed.

Enter Matt Winn.

At the time a Louisville tailor, he had no previous experience in racetrack operations, but he still had the imagination and the determination to take on the assignment of providing Churchill Downs with a face-lift and the Derby with a liftoff.

Winn was told of the track's plight by former Churchill Downs official Charles F. Price in the late summer of 1902. Price pleaded with Winn to buy the Churchill Downs property.

"I've been all over town trying to get a buyer," Price told Winn. "No one wants it. I'm trying you as the last resort. Buy it and keep the Derby alive. If you don't, the Derby dies. Those fellows have lost as much as they care to lose. They won't carry on any further."

Winn wasn't particularly fond of the idea of entering into a business venture that could lead to financial trouble for himself, but on the other hand the preservation of the Derby was of extreme importance to him. With the Derby's fate seemingly in his hands, Winn helped form a syndicate of Louisvillians to put up forty thousand dollars to purchase the track.

Charles F. Grainger, mayor of Louisville, was named track president and Winn vice president. Winn kept his tailor shop in operation the first year his group owned the track, but in late 1903 he was asked by Grainger and others to take over duties as Downs general manager.

Winn initially expressed reluctance to launch a new career at the age of forty-two, but eventually he agreed to leave his tailoring profession and run the show at the Downs. It didn't really matter that he had no background in racetrack management because, as Winn put it, "I didn't know anything about clothing when I became a tailor. I'm a great beginner."

He was more than a great beginner. First and foremost, Winn was a great promoter. And it turned out that he was just the right man to come along at this time to try to give the faltering Derby a shot in the arm. He had the mind of a businessman and the flair of a publicity man. He was a personable individual whom a friend once described as "the only Irish diplomat in existence." But Winn could be a fighter, too. Whenever a business battle erupted, Winn was never afraid to step in and go to war.

If ever there was a man ahead of his time in the field of promotion, it was Matt Winn, who was born in Louisville on June 30, 1861. He quit St. Xavier High School at the age of fourteen and attended business school at night. From there he worked several months as an assistant bookkeeper for a glass company, then went into the grocery business, and later became a traveling salesman for a wholesale house. He then turned to tailoring.

Winn had always been a fan of the Derby. As a freckle-faced boy of thirteen, he watched the inaugural running in 1875 from the seat of his father's flat-bed grocery wagon in the infield, and he never missed a Derby thereafter for the rest of his life. Prior to his employment at the Downs, he put five dollars on two 100–1 outsiders on the same afternoon. Both won.

When Winn's group took over the Downs in 1902, the Derby was not receiving the local support that it once did from prominent Louisvillians. The new management decided to build a thirty-thousand-dollar frame clubhouse, financing it by offering membership to the clubhouse to two hundred high-ranking Louisvillians at a cost of a hundred dollars each. Leading up to the 1903 Derby, *The Louisville Herald* described the clubhouse in this fashion: "A broad veranda encircles the building, and the portion fronting the track is filled with easy benches and chairs.

On the roof there is a magnificent promenade. The main cafe, which opens on the front veranda with colonial doors and windows, is furnished with oak. A massive red brick fireplace is screened with palms and ferns, and all over the spacious hall are clusters of palms and ferns."

The *Kentucky Irish American*, a weekly publication that sold for five cents per issue or one dollar for a year's subscription, said: "The sport under the management of the New Louisville Club promises to be better than ever. The grand stand has been repainted and the old wooden boxes have given place to handsome ones of iron. The new club house is a thing of beauty."

After going to work at the Downs, Winn gave up gambling—on horses, that is. Convinced that the powerful Western Turf Association was awarding unfavorable dates to the Downs, Winn took a gamble in 1904. He defected from that group and joined with nine other discontented tracks to form the American Turf Association. The new group, headed by Winn, proceeded to stage an all-out attack, conducting race meetings in direct competition with important rival tracks. In the end, Winn's group won out.

Winn went from a newcomer to racetrack operations in 1902 to a man known throughout the industry in five short years. By 1907, he was president of the American Turf Association, an organization that controlled all of the tracks in the South and Midwest. Moreover, he was general manager of five tracks—the New Louisville Jockey Club (Churchill Downs), Douglas Park in Louisville, Empire City in Yonkers, New York, and the Crescent City Jockey Club and City Park, both in New Orleans.

One of the most important battles that he fought in his early days at Churchill Downs came in 1908 when a new city administration, one that was hostile to track president Grainger, arranged to have a law passed that made bookmaking illegal. Consequently, the 1908 Derby faced the threat of cancellation because, at the time, bookmaking had been the only form of betting in use at the Downs for many years.

Winn had his back to the wall, but he wasn't about to give up. He discovered an old amendment stating that the pari-mutuel and auction pool forms of wagering were legal in Kentucky. Winn proceeded to round up eleven old pari-mutuel machines, but even then the battle still hadn't been won. City Hall, paying no attention to the amendment, threatened to arrest anyone involved in public wagering of any kind at the Downs. The Downs, though, was successful in obtaining a restraining order that prevented interference with the opening of its spring meeting. The show went on. The 1908 Derby was run on schedule.

Pari-mutuel wagering, all but ignored in America for more than thirty years, spread from the Downs after the Derby. In a revolutionary racing development, this form of wagering eventually became accepted throughout the country.

Winn was fighting on other fronts, too. In New York, he had joined with James Butler to start a race meeting at Empire City. The Jockey Club originally opposed the thoroughbred track, but the tenacious Winn made Empire City a quick success.

In 1909, Winn and Butler expanded their operation south of the border down Mexico way, where they coddled the notorious Pancho Villa and persuaded him to assert his authority in assuring that the Juarez race meeting would be run without any outside trouble.

Villa was well rewarded for his efforts. He remained on Winn's payroll for years, as did several sportswriters. One of those writers was Hy Schneider.

Oscar Otis, late writer for the *Daily Racing Form*, once noted that "after Winn's death, it was discovered that he had an annual annuity to Schneider and while nobody knew what it was all about, it nevertheless was paid as Winn had decreed."

Otis said that an investigation "out of curiosity" some years after Winn's death revealed that "Schneider had saved Winn's life in the brawling days of Juarez and this was his way of expressing his eternal gratitude."

Otis recalled that Winn was "a true friend" to the press "in fair weather and bad, and he really did have the power to convince one that the Derby was indeed the only thing that really mattered in all this world. It was infectious.

"Winn was always personally available to the press," Otis added. "He liked newspapermen, was witty, treated them like kings, gave them the run of the backstretch to do their own news digging. Moreover, he was a rather courtly and distinguished personality, but he did not have a trace of snobbery. He really felt that all men are equal on the turf and acted as if he believed it."

During his career, the dynamic Winn supervised many racetracks. Besides Churchill Downs, Douglas Park, Empire City, Crescent City, and City Park, he was associated with Lincoln Fields, Washington Park, Laurel Park, Latonia, Lexington, Fairmount Park, Juarez, Mexico City, and others. Through it all, the Kentucky Derby remained his abiding interest.

It took Winn time before he was able to get the Derby rolling into high gear. Through his early years at the Downs, the Derby was still a provincial event for the most part, but by 1911 it was beginning to attract Eastern attention. With New York racing embroiled in a two-year shutdown, Easterner R. F. Carman sent his fine colt, Meridian, to Louisville and won the Derby.

After the 1910 renewal, Winn said: "It was the greatest Derby ever run. It will be remembered for years to come. It was the largest crowd ever at Churchill Downs. Over forty thousand were in attendance, and there was not a single cause for complaint."

After the 1911 Derby, Winn said: "The race was splendid. I predict that the meeting here will be the best that was ever held at Churchill Downs."

As it turned out, 1911 was not a very good year for publicity at Churchill Downs, but the Derby could thank Winn for keeping its skeletons locked in the closet as well as he could. A scandalous cloud was threatening to hang over that particular Derby. Capt. James T. Williams, the stable's boss, whose Governor Gray finished second, implied that his jockey, Roscoe Troxler, pulled the horse. Williams even went so far as to twice attack big-time gambler Charles Ellison with a heavy cane. It seems that the quick-tempered Williams heard that Ellison had wagered heavily on Meridian and had given Troxler money afterward.

Track management did its best to sweep the controversy under the rug in the hope that all would be forgotten.

As Jim Henry wrote in Louisville's *Herald-Post* in 1935, "As a virtual czar at Churchill Downs, Colonel Winn has chaperoned the Derby as gingerly as any Spanish donna over a virginal Seville beauty. For three decades no Derby scandal of any consequence has seeped into print. For many years Colonel Winn successfully bottled the sewer gas fumes arising from the Derby of 1911."

The triumphant Meridian went on to earn acclaim as the best three-year-old of 1911, marking only the second time in twenty-six years that a Derby horse had gained such an honor. The trend toward higher quality of Derby horses continued in 1912, when the race was won by Worth, the first juvenile money leader to run in the event in twenty-three years. Worth was owned by H. C. Hallenbeck of New York, and in 1913 the Derby favorite, Ten Point, similarly was the property of a New Yorker, bootblack king A. L. Aste. Ten Point failed to win the Derby, but the fact that Donerail, ridden by Roscoe Goose, came rolling home at a whopping $184.90 straight payoff didn't hurt the race from a headline standpoint.

The Derby was starting to receive more and more attention, and so was Winn. A 1913 story in the *Daily Racing Form* acknowledged Winn's contributions, saying: "Favored by opportunities and always equal to the mastery of any situation that might present itself, it has been given to Matt J. Winn in the course of a few years past to ascend to a position in connection with racing seldom ever attained. . . . Mr. Winn had been one of those actively instrumental in securing the enactment of the law creating the Kentucky State Racing Commission and in the measure leading to the substitution of the new betting method in place of the old."

Old Rosebud, the country's best two-year-old of 1913, appeared on the Derby scene in 1914 and roared to a blazing victory in 2:03²/₅, breaking the track record set the year before by Donerail. Never at a lost for words when it came to promoting the Derby, Winn said following the 1914 running: "It fulfilled my every expectation. I knew the field this year contained phenomenal three-year-olds, and it was no surprise to me when Old Rosebud, followed in by Hodge, made a new track record for a mile and a quarter at the Downs. As to the crowd, it was far in excess of any throng that ever witnessed a race in Kentucky."

The longshot and track-record victory by Donerail in 1913, coupled with Old Rosebud's 1914 triumph in track-record time, served as a parlay that Winn made good use of in promoting widespread publicity for the Derby. In 1915, newspaper advertising leading up to the Derby heralded the event as "America's greatest race." But if the race indeed did stand taller than any other in the country, it did so on shaky grounds. The Derby still needed to be strengthened, still needed the finishing touches applied to its ever-gaining popularity. And along came Regret.

Some veteran racing followers believe that the importance of this filly's Derby triumph is overplayed, but Winn, in recalling the 1915 renewal years later, said that the race "needed only a victory by Regret to create for us some coast-to-coast publicity, and Regret did not fail us. The Derby thus was made as an American institution."

The Derby, to be sure, was on its rosy way, but Winn didn't sit still. He kept after the major stables to bring their contenders to the Derby.

The 1922 Derby was another example of Winn's promotional work.

Morvich was the unbeaten two-year-old champion of 1921, a horse mentioned at the time in the same breath with Man o' War. The Derby that year was run on the same day as the Preakness. Would Morvich go to Baltimore rather than Louisville?

Winn declared two months before the Derby that Morvich would run for the roses.

Winn didn't stay home in ol' Kentucky and wait for Morvich and other outstanding horses to come to him. He went to New York and discussed the Derby with a number of horsemen, including, of course, Ben Block, the Wall Street financier who owned Morvich. Predicting that the 1922 renewal would be "the greatest Derby ever run," Winn returned to Kentucky and said, "I just came from New York and while there received the assurance of Benjamin Block that he would send Morvich here to run in the Derby. Mr. Block has already made hotel reservations for his party and engaged stable room for his stable at Churchill Downs."

As promised, Morvich was delivered to Louisville for the Derby. Although he later proved to be vastly overrated, Morvich won the Derby, and out-of-town reporters converged on the Downs in great numbers to write about the heralded colt. The New York press covered the 1922 race like a blanket. *The New York Times* and *New York Morning Telegraph* even put Morvich's Derby victory on page one, as did the *Tribune* and *World*.

Winn's comments about the 1922 Derby were predictable: "It was the greatest Derby Day we have ever enjoyed. It was the biggest crowd ever in Churchill Downs; and what a cosmopolitan crowd it was! Notables from all over America were present, and, besides, every section of the nation was represented by the men of modest means whose love for the thoroughbred caused them to make the pilgrimage. The popularity of racing with the American people was illustrated well by the assemblage at the Downs. I think it fitting that a super horse such as Morvich should be crowned on such an occasion."

In the ensuing years, Winn encountered few problems as he directed the Derby to continuing success. One trouble spot did arise in 1943. That year's Derby was known as "Winn's Win."

Early in the year *The Thoroughbred Record* reported: " . . . it was Colonel Matt Winn, grizzled veteran of war, fire, flood and famine, who restored some semblance of order by announcing that the Kentucky Derby would be held this year."

The Derby, it seems, was threatened with cancellation because of transportation restrictions brought about by the United States' involvement in World War II. The Derby, at the time, relied on special trains to carry fans to Louisville, and Joseph B. Eastman, an official with the Office of Defense Transportation, issued a statement that said: "It would be better from a transportation standpoint if the Kentucky Derby were not run this year."

Winn had something to say about the matter himself. The Derby would *not* be canceled, declared Winn, who stressed that Churchill Downs would do all in its power to discourage nonresidents of the Louisville area from attending the 1943 running. "The Kentucky Derby will be run, even if there are only two horses in the race and only two people in the stands," Winn declared.

Eastman conceded and put his stamp of approval on the

race. "Matt Winn's scrapping already had wiped out one threat to the Derby, even before the Office of Defense Transportation started sniping at it," stated *The Thoroughbred Record*. "A few days before, William Jeffers, national rubber administrator, had decreed that no race meetings could be conducted at tracks accessible mainly by automobile. This, he asserted, was in the interest of tire conservation. For Churchill Downs, that problem was solved by agreeing to close the plant's parking lots and to discourage fans from coming to the track by motor."

Winn went about the business of asking out-of-town Derby boxholders to turn over their tickets to members of the armed forces stationed near Louisville. A crowd of 61,209, made up predominantly of Louisvillians, attended the 1943 Derby. That race and the 1944 renewal were known as the "Streetcar Derbies."

Since then, the Derby has prospered, thanks entirely to the foundation laid by Winn, a chubby, pink-faced, cigar-smoking Kentuckian who was best described as looking "something like Alfred Hitchcock, with a bit of W. C. Fields thrown in."

Winn, whose wife died in 1912, lived for years in a six-room apartment at Churchill Downs. Late in his life, he would wander around his beloved plant during the off season. Followed by a valet carrying a cane-bottom chair, Winn frequently would stop and sit so as to study the track's facilities and landscaping. He was always looking for ways to make improvements.

To the end, Winn never tired of discussing the Derby. "Winn lived the Derby for 24 hours a day," Jerry McNerney of *The Courier-Journal* once wrote. "He slept with it, he ate with it and he talked it to anybody who'd listen."

Winn looked forward to seeing the Diamond Jubilee Derby in 1949, making plans for the race some four years in advance. In 1947, he overcame a serious illness and went on with his preparations for the seventy-fifth Derby. A man with incredible stamina and vitality, Winn lived to see the 1949 Derby, which was won by Calumet Farm's Ponder.

Known as "Mr. Derby," he had seen the first seventy-five Derbies, from Aristides in 1875 through Ponder in 1949, and the Diamond Jubilee running was to be his last. He passed away on October 6, 1949, at the age of eighty-eight.

Following Winn's death, Frank Jennings wrote in *The Thoroughbred Record* magazine: "The fine old Kentucky Colonel was typical of the tradition of his title, and was admired by practically everybody who came in contact with him. He always was ready with a yarn for writers and newsmen and with straight bourbon or juleps for his guests."

Damon Runyon wrote of Winn: "The sports writing fraternity is in his debt . . . for affording it a subject of never failing interest to newspaper readers from the time the last leaf falls in autumn until the buds come again in the spring.

"I have known a great many men in sport in my time. I have known the champions and the promoters. I have known the magnates and the moguls. I have known those who could take the good and the bad with the same kind of a smile, and I have known the cry babies—the ones who could not stand up when the going got tough. But of them all, I have never known one who has worn as well as Colonel Winn."

Ferdinand, the 1986 Kentucky Derby winner, edged Alysheba, the 1987 Derby winner, in the 1987 Breeders' Cup Classic at Hollywood Park. (Courtesy Breeders' Cup)

5

Matching Up Those Derby Winners

WHEN TWO KENTUCKY DERBY winners square off against each other, it somehow seems only fitting that they should finish one-two.

That's what Alysheba and Ferdinand did in three of their four encounters.

Indeed, one-two finishes between Derby kings have taken place in nine of the past twelve races that have brought together winners of America's premier horse race.

But that hasn't always been the trend, these one-two finishes between Derby winners. In the first such thirty-one meetings, starting with Ben Ali's victory over third-place finisher Joe Cotton in an 1887 race, all the way up to the 1950 Hollywood Gold Cup (Ponder came in fourth, Assault seventh), only five times did Derby winners run first and second.

Then the one-two trend began in 1955 with Swaps winning the Californian Stakes and Determine running second.

Over the years, there have been five one-two finishes between Derby winners decided by a half-length or less, and three of those involved Alysheba and Ferdinand.

In 1897, Plaudit, who was to win the 1898 Derby, captured an all-age race as a two-year-old, and Ben Brush, the 1896 Derby champion, ran second. In 1923, Exterminator edged Paul Jones by a neck to win the Philadelphia Handicap.

And then there were the three Alysheba-Ferdinand duels to the wire.

In the 1987 Breeders' Cup Classic, Ferdinand triumphed by a nose over Alysheba. With Bill Shoemaker timing his move perfectly, the favored Ferdinand moved past Judge Angelucci and then held off the late charge by Alysheba in the mile-and-a-quarter race.

"I didn't want to make the lead too soon," Shoemaker said, "but I was kind of worried at about the sixteenth pole whether I was going to get by the Judge or not. I saw Alysheba coming up on the outside, and I just waited, waited, waited, then I shook my stick at him and let him go to the lead. He saw Alysheba coming in just enough time to put in a little extra effort, and he got the job done."

The Classic marked the first time that two Derby winners had finished one-two in the same race with only a whisker separating them. But it wouldn't be the last.

The next year, Alysheba would win out in a nose verdict over Ferdinand. But before that race the favored Alysheba won the mile-and-a-quarter Santa Anita Handicap by a half-length over Ferdinand. Then, in the mile-and-an-eighth San Bernardino Handicap, Alysheba triumphed by a nose over Ferdinand. Alysheba was favored at 4–5, with Ferdinand the even-money second choice.

In the fourth and final meeting between these two rivals, neither triumphed. Cutlass Reality won the mile-and-a-quarter Hollywood Gold Cup Handicap by six and a half lengths over Alysheba, the even-money favorite. It was another five and a half lengths back to Ferdinand in third.

In their four encounters, Alysheba held a 3–1 advantage over Ferdinand.

Triple Crown Battles

Triple Crown winners twice have raced against each other, and both times Seattle Slew got the best of Affirmed.

Their first meeting, the 1978 Marlboro Cup at Belmont Park, was headlined "A Clash of Crowns." Affirmed was favored at 1–2 and carried 124 pounds. Seattle Slew, for the only time in his career, was not favored. He was the 2.10–1 second choice in the field of six.

Ridden for the first time by Angel Cordero Jr. and with 128 up, Seattle Slew took the lead at the start and controlled the pace with a first quarter of a mile in twenty-four seconds and the half-mile in :47. Affirmed was running second—but was trailing by too much, as far as his trainer, Laz Barrera, was concerned. Seattle Slew stayed in front the entire way, hitting the finish line three lengths ahead of second-place Affirmed and running the mile and one-eighth in 1:45⁴/₅, just two-fifths of a second off Secretariat's world record set in the 1973 Marlboro.

Barrera questioned Steve Cauthen's ride aboard Affirmed. "You just don't go twenty-four, forty-seven," Barrera said. "Impossible. I told him (Cauthen) to stay one length away at most off that horse—the only one he had to beat. On a straightway, twenty-four, forty-seven, you can't do that."

Columnist Mike Barry of *The Louisville Times* disagreed with Barrera. "If you watched the race," Barry wrote, "you know Cauthen started sending Affirmed at the three-eighths pole, not waiting until the two were straightened away in the stretch. Steve had Affirmed in an all-out drive for the final three furlongs—and never gained an inch. Seattle Slew was just too much horse."

Seattle Slew so impressed Cordero that the veteran jockey said, "I've never been around a horse of this class. It's like flying an airplane.

"I beat a great combination—a great horse, a great trainer and a great owner," Cordero added. "There'll probably be a rematch, but I got the biggie. We're No. 1."

There was a rematch, Seattle Slew and Affirmed meeting again a month later in the Jockey Club Gold Cup at Belmont Park.

Even though neither Derby winner triumphed in this race, Seattle Slew demonstrated his genuine quality. After six furlongs in 1:09²/₅, a clocking that track announcer Chic Anderson described to a national television audience as "unbelievable" in a mile-and-a-half race, Seattle Slew would have had every right to call it quits against Exceller, who had come with a rush from far off the pace. Exceller took the lead in the stretch, but Seattle Slew dug in and battled back in a remarkable effort. At the wire, it was Exceller by a nose.

Seattle Slew was lauded in defeat. "Slew, even in losing, came up with a true-grit performance that proved his class and courage beyond doubt," sports editor Billy Reed wrote in *The Courier-Journal*.

As for Affirmed, he had an excuse in this race. His saddle slipped, and he wound up finishing a distant fifth in an effort that should be disregarded in judging this brilliant runner's career.

Affirmed came back in the 1979 Jockey Club Gold Cup and triumphed by three-quarters of a length over Spectacular Bid, that year's Derby winner. The victory nailed down Affirmed's second straight Horse of the Year championship.

"You can't take nothing away from Spectacular Bid," said Barrera, the proud trainer of Affirmed. "He is a hell of a horse. Spectacular Bid is a great horse, but Affirmed is a little better. Affirmed is a super horse, the best in America or in Europe. I don't want to insult nobody, but Affirmed is the best horse I ever saw."

Grover "Bud" Delp, the trainer of Spectacular Bid, had his own opinion. "The pace makes the race," he said. "No horse has ever lived who can give Affirmed the lead in :49 (for the first half) and then get by him. If Bid had the lead and had gone a half in :49, there's no horse living who could have gotten by him either. Affirmed went three-quarters in thirteen and one (1:13¹/₅). Hell, ten thousand horses can do that."

Just as he had disagreed with Barrera after the 1978 Marlboro, Barry took issue with Delp.

"What rubbish!" Barry wrote in *The Louisville Times*. "If Affirmed had such an advantage going the first half in :49, why didn't Spectacular Bid go in :48⁴/₅? Then the 3-year-old would have had the lead. And, according to his trainer, no horse living could have gotten by him.

"True, 10,000 horses can go three-quarters in 1:13¹/₅— *if* they're only going three-quarters, and *if* they're running with other 1:13¹/₅ horses, and *if* they won't have to go three-quarters more against Affirmed."

Barry went on to praise Spectacular Bid for being the talented horse that he was. "Spectacular Bid is as game as he is fast," Barry wrote. "In the stretch drive, when he was between Affirmed and Coastal, he tried every yard. The 3-year-old couldn't get to Affirmed (I thought at the eighth pole he was going to do it) but it didn't stop him from trying.

"The Bid's a fine racehorse. He is not, obviously, the greatest horse that ever looked through a bridle, as Delp insisted last winter. But he's a runner—it took Affirmed's best to beat him."

Delp later called for a rematch with Affirmed, but none was forthcoming.

"I want a match race with Affirmed more than I want to be with my girlfriend in Las Vegas," the outspoken trainer said after Spectacular Bid's victory later that fall in the Meadowlands Cup.

In an interview the following year, Delp said, "I begged for a rematch, and they turned around and went home. The Horse of the Year was more important to them than drawing a television audience of maybe 30 million. It would have been great for racing. Of course, I can't say I blame them, because they'd have finished second."

That was Bud Delp's opinion.

Clash of Triple Derby Winners

On two occasions, three Derby winners have run against each other—the 1917 Brooklyn Handicap (Regret, Old Rosebud, and Omar Khayyam) and the 1918 Bowie Handicap (George Smith, Omar Khayyam, and Exterminator).

The 1917 Brooklyn Handicap matched one of the greatest fields in racing history. The eleven contestants included:

•Regret, 1915 Kentucky Derby winner who was considered the best two-year-old filly of 1914, America's leading racehorse of 1915, and the top female handicap horse of 1917.

•Old Rosebud, 1914 Kentucky Derby winner who earned recognition as the top two-year-old male of 1913 and America's best racehorse of 1917.

•Omar Khayyam, 1917 Kentucky Derby winner who shared acclaim with Hourless as the season's most outstanding male three-year-olds.

•Roamer, who was regarded as the finest horse in the country in 1914 and was rated best male handicap runner of 1915, an honor that he shared with Short Grass in 1916.

•Borrow, who was ranked with Great Britain as the best handicap male horses of 1914.

Regret and Borrow were owned by Harry Payne Whitney and trained by Jimmy Rowe. Willie Knapp, who rode

Borrow, asked Rowe before the race about the stable's game plan. Rowe informed Knapp that Whitney preferred to win with Regret but that he had better be ready with Borrow in case the likes of Old Rosebud or Roamer threatened.

Regret was hurried into the early lead and held off one challenge after another. Borrow, meanwhile, was running seventh in the early going. With Old Rosebud looming a serious threat, Knapp then drove Borrow through on the inside in the stretch. Trouble was, once he drove past Old Rosebud, he didn't apply the brakes. In the late going, Borrow overtook Regret and won by a margin reported as a nose or a head.

Frank Robinson, who rode Regret, perhaps figured that he had the race won in the final sixteenth. After all, at the stretch call, Regret led by a length and a half over Borrow, and it was no secret which of his two horses Whitney wanted to win. Robinson, apparently thinking that Knapp would not try to beat Regret with Borrow, "took matters easy in the last sixteenth," according to the footnotes in the *Daily Racing Form*'s chart—and the result was a victory for Borrow.

Borrow ran the mile and one-eighth in 1:49^2/$_5$, listed as an American record in the chart but reported in certain other publications as a world record. The former record was 1:49^3/$_5$, which Regret also bettered. Afterward, Whitney either cried or came close to it.

One story said that the Brooklyn "will be long remembered by the thousands who witnessed it. While Harry Payne Whitney's aged gelding Borrow, carrying 117 pounds, won the event, his stablemate, the chestnut mare Regret, winner of the Kentucky Derby of 1915, was the heroine of the race. From flag fall to within fifty yards of the finish this 5-year-old daughter of Broomstock-Jersey Lightning led the field of eleven of the best horses in America, setting such a dizzy pace that the winner's time, 1:49^2/$_5$, sets a new world's record for the distance."

Omar Khayyam, who beat only one horse in the 1917 Brooklyn Handicap, finished behind only one horse in the 1918 Bowie Handicap, the other race that featured three Kentucky Derby winners. George Smith, packing high weight of 130 pounds, clipped three-fifths of a second off the Pimlico track record for a mile and a half in winning the Bowie Handicap. He triumphed by three-quarters of a length over Omar Khayyam, who was half a length in front of third-place Exterminator. Thus, all three Derby winners ran the race in faster time than the existing track record of 2:31⁴/₅.

Running Against a Derby Winner

Not all of these forty-three races were billed as matchups of Kentucky Derby winners. In three cases, one of the horses involved hadn't yet won the Derby.

A week before Macbeth II was to win the 1888 Derby he faced Montrose, who had captured the Derby a year earlier. Macbeth II finished second in the Distillers' Stakes at Lexington while Montrose came in fourth. Montrose carried 118 pounds, compared with ninety-four on Macbeth II.

In three other 1888 meetings, Montrose crossed the finish line in front of Macbeth II. Montrose gave Macbeth II weight each time, twelve pounds in one, four or nine in another, sixteen in the last. Montrose's 3–1 advantage over Macbeth II supported the old adage that a good four-year-old will beat a good three-year-old.

Altogether, sixteen of the forty-three Derby winner-versus-Derby winner races have put a three-year-old who had, or would, win the Derby against a four-year-old Derby victor. The four-year-olds outran the sophomores in all but four of the sixteen races.

For a three-year-old to run against a four-year-old is one

thing, but a juvenile competing with—and *beating*—an older horse is something else. Back in the Gay Nineties, the two-year-old Plaudit, destined to win the 1898 Derby, carried a feathery ninety pounds to a narrow victory over Ben Brush, the 1896 Derby king packing 126 pounds. The race took place at the old Gravesend track in Brooklyn.

Ben Brush, who conceded twelve to thirty-six pounds to his four opponents, went off as an odds-on favorite. Plaudit took the lead early in the race and won in a close finish over Ben Brush and Dr. Catlett, a three-year-old who had finished third in the 1897 Kentucky Derby. Plaudit's winning margin was a head or a neck over Ben Brush, who in turn was just a head in front of Dr. Catlett.

"When the fourth race at Gravesend to-day had been run the crowd stood aghast," stated one news account. "The great Ben Brush, who could beat anybody's horse a few days ago and was in the pink of condition then, had his colors lowered by a two-year-old, and a lame one at that, and one that had not shown much of anything in his last race."

Plaudit, listed at odds of 40–1 and 50–1, covered the mile and a sixteenth in 1:47½. *The Thoroughbred Record* magazine reported that after the race Plaudit was roundly cheered by the crowd of eight thousand or more, "mostly all of whom had bet on either Ben Brush or Dr. Catlett. . . . Plaudit's race had been such as to command the respect of the great crowd, and as for the horsemen present the colt's performance almost took their breath away. Notwithstanding the fact that Brush and Dr. Catlett were strongly played some nice bunches of money went in on Plaudit."

The other horse to run against a Derby winner before he himself had won the Derby was Elwood. In late February of his three-year-old season, more than two months before he was to win the Derby, Elwood ran in a mile-and-a-sixteenth race that carried a four-hundred-dollar purse. Among his opponents in the field of five was His Eminence, the 1901 Derby winner. Neither horse distinguished himself in this race at Los Angeles. His Eminence finished fourth, five lengths ahead of Elwood. The chart's footnotes said: "His Eminence showed speed on the home turn, but on the whole ran a bad race. Elwood retired early."

Exterminator Lives Up to His Name

No Derby winner raced as often against Derby winners as Exterminator did. Exterminator, who squared off against Omar Khayyam, George Smith, Sir Barton, and Paul Jones, competed in fourteen of these races, meeting Derby winners fifteen times in the process. (He faced George Smith and Omar Khayyam in the 1918 Bowie Handicap.) Exterminator finished ahead of the other Derby winners in nine of the fifteen races that he ran against them. A great weight carrier, Exterminator had more pounds on his back than his fellow Derby winners in twelve of those fifteen encounters.

Exterminator and Paul Jones were longtime rivals, meeting ten times from 1920 to 1923. In every race, Exterminator carried much more weight than Paul Jones—193½ more pounds, to be exact, an average difference of better than nineteen pounds per meeting. Exterminator finished ahead of Paul Jones in all but three of their ten confrontations.

In one of his races against Paul Jones, the two-and-a-fourth-mile Pimlico Cup Handicap of 1920, Exterminator carried 126 pounds to a track-record victory of 3:53. Boniface, who ran second under 114 pounds, was edged by Exterminator in a thrilling finish while Paul Jones, 110½, came in a distant third, ten lengths back.

Derby Winners Duel at the Downs

On two occasions, Derby winners have faced each other at Churchill Downs, the site of the Derby.

The first time the race carried a meager twenty-two-hundred-dollar purse.

The second time the race was worth $3 million.

The first race obviously was not of a championship variety. On May 16, 1930, the day before Gallant Fox won the Kentucky Derby, Whiskery and Clyde Van Dusen were among a field of ten horses who went to the post in the Shady Brook Farm Handicap, an easily forgettable mile-and-a-sixteenth race. Clyde Van Dusen, who went off as the third choice at 4.28–1 odds, finished dead last. Whiskery, dismissed at 85.82–1, came in second, missing by a neck of catching Easter Stockings, a five-year-old daughter of Sir Barton.

The second meeting between Derby winners at Churchill Downs took place on November 2, 1991, in the Breeders' Cup Classic. Unbridled, in the final start of his career, rallied from last place to finish third at 4.30–1 odds, beaten three and three-quarters lengths for all the marbles. More than a few observers believed that he might have won the Classic had the front-running winner, Black Tie Affair, not been allowed to set the slowest early fractions (:24$^{1/5}$, :48$^{2/5}$ and 1:12$^{3/5}$) in the race's history. "Black Tie Affair ran a great race and deserved to win," said Carl Nafzger, the trainer of Unbridled, "but I think our horse ran a winning race."

As for Strike the Gold, the 6.20–1 shot came on to finish fifth in the field of eleven.

Riva Ridge's "Indignity"

One Derby winner suffered the indignity of losing in his only meeting with the Derby winner of the previous year and losing his lone race against the Derby winner of the following year. That horse was Riva Ridge, who couldn't beat the older Canonero II in the 1972 Stymie Handicap or the younger Secretariat in the 1973 Marlboro Cup. Riva Ridge was second in both races.

Well, maybe it wasn't an indignity, after all, to lose these two races. Riva Ridge's conquerors either equaled or set a world record. Canonero II won the Stymie in 1:46$\frac{1}{5}$, equaling a world record on the dirt for the mile-and-an-eighth distance. Secretariat captured the Marlboro in 1:45$\frac{2}{5}$, setting a world record on the dirt for a mile and one-eighth and equaling the mark that Tentam had achieved on the grass at that distance the previous month.

Running All Over

Of the forty-three races, seventeen have been run in the state of New York, nine in California, nine in Maryland, six in Kentucky, one in Illinois, and one in Canada.

RACE (distance)	DATE, TRACK	DERBY WINNERS	(AGE . . . WT.)	FINISH
Free Handicap Sweepstakes (1 1/16 miles)	Oct. 7, 1887 Jerome Park	Ben Ali Joe Cotton	(4 . . . 118) (5 . . . 112)	1st 3rd
Distillers' Stakes (1 1/4 miles)	May 7, 1888 Kentucky Assoc. (Lexington)	Macbeth II Montrose	(3 . . . 94) (4 . . . 118)	2nd 4th
Distillers' and Brewers' Stakes (1 mile & 500 yards)	June 2, 1888 Latonia	Montrose Macbeth II	(4 . . . 115) (3 . . . 103)	1st 3rd
Boulevard Stakes (1 1/4 miles)	July 3, 1888 Washington Park	Montrose Macbeth II	(4 . . . 113 or 118) (3 . . . 109)	2nd 6th
Handicap Sweepstakes (1 1/2 miles)	Aug. 18, 1888 Saratoga	Montrose Macbeth II	(4 . . . 118) (3 . . . 102)	1st 4th
All-age race (1 1/16 miles)	Sept. 29, 1897 Gravesend	Plaudit Ben Brush	(2 . . . 90) (4 . . . 126)	1st 2nd

RACE (distance)	DATE, TRACK	DERBY WINNERS	(AGE . . . WT.)	FINISH
Selling race	Feb. 24, 1904	His Eminence	(6 . . . 104)	4th
$400 purse	Los Angeles	Elwood	(3 . . . 101	5th
(1 1/16 miles)	Jockey Club		or 102)	
Handicap for 3 & up	June 5, 1905	Alan-a-Dale	(6 . . . 122)	4th
(1 1/16 miles)	Gravesend	Elwood	(4 . . . 104)	8th
Brewers' Exchange	June 25, 1910	Wintergreen	(4 . . . 117)	3rd
Handicap	Latonia	Donau	(3 . . . 112)	8th
(six furlongs)				
Handicap for 3 & up	Aug. 12, 1912	Worth	(3 . . . 119)	3rd
(six furlongs)	Hamilton,	Wintergreen	(6 . . . 113)	5th
	Ontario			
Douglas Park				
Inaugural Handicap	Sept. 16, 1912	Wintergreen	(6 . . . 107)	8th
(1 1/16 miles)	Douglas Park	Donau	(5 . . . 106)	left at
	(Louisville)			post
Brooklyn Handicap	June 25, 1917	Regret	(5 . . . 122)	2nd
(1 1/8 miles)	Aqueduct	Old Rosebud	(6 . . . 120)	3rd
		Omar Khayyam	(3 . . . 110)	10th
Saratoga Handicap	Aug. 1, 1917	George Smith	(4 . . . 117)	4th
(1 1/4 miles)	Saratoga	Old Rosebud	(6 . . . 132)	5th
Washington Handicap	Oct. 12, 1918	Exterminator	(3 . . . 113 1/2)	3rd
(1 1/8 miles)	Laurel Park	Omar Khayyam	(4 . . . 127)	4th
Bowie Handicap	Nov. 12, 1918	George Smith	(5 . . . 130)	1st
(1 1/2 miles)	Pimlico	Omar Khayyam	(4 . . . 115)	2nd
		Exterminator	(3 . . . 120)	3rd
Havre de Grace	Sept. 27, 1919	Exterminator	(4 . . . 126)	2nd
Handicap	Havre de Grace	Sir Barton	(3 . . . 124)	3rd
(1 1/8 miles)				
Suburban Handicap	June 5, 1920	Paul Jones	(3 . . . 106)	1st
(1 1/4 miles)	Belmont Park	Exterminator	(5 . . . 123)	3rd
Saratoga Handicap	Aug. 2, 1920	Sir Barton	(4 . . . 129)	1st
(1 1/4 miles)	Saratoga	Exterminator	(5 . . . 126)	2nd

RACE (distance)	DATE, TRACK	DERBY WINNERS	(AGE . . . WT.)	FINISH
Bowie Handicap	Nov. 8, 1920	Paul Jones	(3 . . . 120)	4th
(1 1/2 miles)	Pimlico	Exterminator	(5 . . . 135)	5th
Pimlico Cup Handicap	Nov. 12, 1920	Exterminator	(5 . . . 126)	1st
(2 1/4 miles)	Pimlico	Paul Jones	(3 . . . 110 1/2)	3rd
Suburban Handicap	June 4, 1921	Exterminator	(6 . . . 133)	5th
(1 1/4 miles)	Belmont Park	Paul Jones	(4 . . . 118)	8th
Brooklyn Handicap	June 17, 1921	Exterminator	(6 . . . 129)	3rd
(1 1/8 miles)	Aqueduct	Paul Jones	(4 . . . 116)	10th
Merchants and	Aug. 27, 1921	Exterminator	(6 . . . 130)	1st
Citizens' Hdcp.	Saratoga	Paul Jones	(4 . . . 109)	5th
(1 3/16 miles)				
Washington Handicap	Oct. 28, 1922	Exterminator	(7 . . . 132)	4th
(1 1/4 miles)	Laurel Park	Paul Jones	(5 . . . 106)	7th
Pimlico Cup Handicap	Nov. 11, 1922	Paul Jones	(5 . . . 99)	2nd
(2 1/4 miles)	Pimlico	Exterminator	(7 . . . 126)	3rd
Philadelphia Handicap	April 21, 1923	Exterminator	(8 . . . 129)	1st
(1 1/16 miles)	Havre de Grace	Paul Jones	(6 . . . 109)	2nd
Old Dominion Handicap	April 28, 1923	Exterminator	(8 . . . 132)	2nd
(1 mile & 70 yards)	Havre de Grace	Paul Jones	(6 . . . 108)	3rd
Shady Brook Farm				
Handicap	May 16, 1930	Whiskery	(6 . . . 108)	2nd
(1 1/16 miles)	Churchill Downs	Clyde Van Dusen	(4 . . . 112)	10th
San Antonio Handicap	Feb. 11, 1950	Ponder	(4 . . . 128)	1st
(1 1/8 miles)	Santa Anita Park	Citation	(5 . . . 130)	2nd
Santa Anita Handicap	Feb. 25, 1950	Citation	(5 . . . 132)	2nd
(1 1/4 miles)	Santa Anita Park	Ponder	(4 . . . 124)	4th
Hollywood Gold Cup	Dec. 9, 1950	Ponder	(4 . . . 125)	5th
(1 1/4 miles)	Hollywood Park	Assault	(7 . . . 121)	7th
Californian Stakes	June 11, 1955	Swaps	(3 . . . 115)	1st
(1 1/16 miles)	Hollywood Park	Determine	(4 . . . 126)	2nd
Schenectady Purse	Aug. 6, 1964	Chateaugay	(4 . . . 124)	1st
(seven furlongs)	Saratoga	Decidedly	(5 . . . 124)	2nd

RACE (distance)	DATE, TRACK	DERBY WINNERS	(AGE . . . WT.)	FINISH
Stymie Handicap	Sept. 20, 1972	Canonero II	(4 . . . 110)	1st
(1 1/8 miles)	Belmont Park	Riva Ridge	(3 . . . 123)	2nd
Marlboro Cup	Sept. 15, 1973	Secretariat	(3 . . . 124)	1st
(1 1/8 miles)	Belmont Park	Riva Ridge	(4 . . . 127)	2nd
Marlboro Cup	Sept. 16, 1978	Seattle Slew	(4 . . . 128)	1st
(1 1/8 miles)	Belmont Park	Affirmed	(3 . . . 124)	2nd
Jockey Club Gold Cup	Oct. 14, 1978	Seattle Slew	(4 . . . 126)	2nd
(1 1/2 miles)	Belmont Park	Affirmed	(3 . . . 121)	5th
Jockey Club Gold Cup	Oct. 6, 1979	Affirmed	(4 . . . 126)	1st
(1 1/2 miles)	Belmont Park	Spectacular Bid	(3 . . . 121)	2nd
Breeders' Cup Classic	Nov. 21, 1987	Ferdinand	(4 . . . 126)	1st
(1 1/4 miles)	Hollywood Park	Alysheba	(3 . . . 122)	2nd
Santa Anita Handicap	March 6, 1988	Alysheba	(4 . . . 126)	1st
(1 1/4 miles)	Santa Anita Park	Ferdinand	(5 . . . 127)	2nd
San Bernardino Handicap	April 17, 1988	Alysheba	(4 . . . 127)	1st
(1 1/8 miles)	Santa Anita Park	Ferdinand	(5 . . . 127)	2nd
Hollywood Gold Cup Handicap	June 26, 1988	Alysheba	(4 . . . 126)	2nd
(1 1/4 miles)	Hollywood Park	Ferdinand	(5 . . . 125)	3rd
Breeders' Cup Classic	Nov. 2, 1991	Unbridled	(4 . . . 126)	3rd
(1 1/4 miles)	Churchill Downs	Strike the Gold	(3 . . . 122)	5th

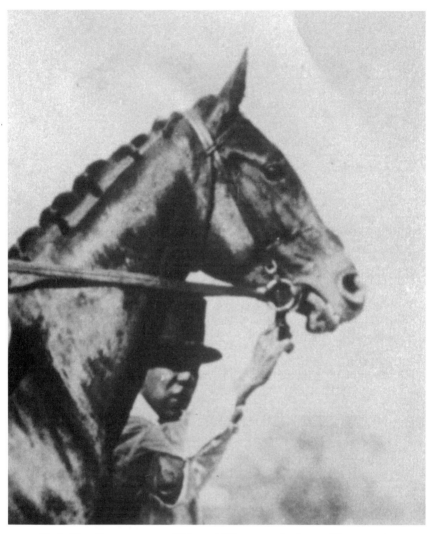

Clyde Van Dusen, a son of Man o' War, was the last gelding to win the Kentucky Derby. He triumphed in 1929. (Courtesy Keeneland Library, Lexington, Kentucky)

6

That Old Gang of Geldings

THEY MAKE UP A SPECIAL CLUB, restricted to guys only.

Just seven members belong to this fraternity, which is made up of geldings who have won the Kentucky Derby. It's been a long time since a new member joined the club. You have to go all the way back to 1929 to find the last gelding who won the Derby—Clyde Van Dusen, a little son of Man o' War.

They were iron horses, those seven geldings. One of them, Macbeth II, raced 106 times in his career. Another, the great Exterminator, went to the post in a hundred races. They kept running and running, but by today's standards they weren't rewarded very well. The seven gelded winners of the Derby collectively raced 536 times in their careers and earned $572,023. By contrast, the Derby has rewarded each of its last seven winners with more purse money than that.

A check of the Derbies from 1960 through 1992 showed that twenty-eight geldings ran for the roses during that time. Only two, Best Pal in 1991 and Bass Clef in 1961, finished in the money. Best Pal ran second to Strike the Gold, beaten a length and three-quarters. Bass Clef finished third in the '61 Derby, which brought together four geldings in the field of fifteen. The other three were Loyal Son (ninth), Ronnie's Ace (thirteenth), and Dearborn (fourteenth).

During that thirty-three-year stretch, two Derbies attracted geldings who later gained Horse of the Year honors. Both finished fourth in the Derby—Roman Brother in 1964 and Forego in 1973. Roman Brother was a 1965 Horse of the Year, while Forego was the best horse in North America for three straight seasons (1974–76). In the last thirty-three Derbies, only one gelding was favored—Rockhill Native, who finished fifth in 1980.

Two interesting notes: The 1920 Derby program listed the victorious Paul Jones as a colt. He was a gelding. And the 1936 Derby program erroneously listed the victorious Bold Venture as a gelding. All Bold Venture did was sire two Derby winners—Assault (1946) and Middleground (1950).

Join us as we roll back the years and take a look at the seven geldings who won the Kentucky Derby, two of whom—Old Rosebud and Exterminator—were good enough to earn a place in racing's Hall of Fame.

Vagrant (1876)

Back when Vagrant won the Derby, geldings carried ninety-seven pounds, three less than colts. Another gelding in the 1876 Derby was Parole, a future Hall of Famer who finished out of the money.

William Astor of New York acquired Vagrant for seven thousand dollars two weeks before the Derby from T. J. Nichols of Paris, Kentucky. Nichols had bought Vagrant for $250 as a yearling. In *The Kentucky Derby Diamond Jubilee* book, George B. "Brownie" Leach wrote that Vagrant's breeder, M. H. Sanford, owned the Derby winner's sire, Virgil, but thought little of him and actually gave him away. "In fact, the man who received Virgil as a gift made a present of him to still another breeder," Leach wrote. "All that happened, however, before Vagrant became the outstanding two-year-old of 1875. When that happened there was a wild scramble on the part of breeders to buy Virgil, and he eventually was sold for $3,500."

Vagrant won the Derby by two lengths, and afterward *The Kentucky Live Stock Record* described him in this fashion: "He has a neat head and neck, good shoulders, excellent middle piece, great length, immense hips and quarters and tremendous stifles, with sound feet and legs. His action is easy and graceful, a regular daisy cutter, and from his style and carriage must go a distance of ground."

Vagrant covered plenty of ground in his racing days, starting eighty-eight times over a nine-year career (1875–83). The last race of his career came in his ten-year-old season. On Sept. 7, 1883, he made his first start since a last-place finish ten months earlier at Jerome Park in New York. In his finale, which drew four horses, the lightly regarded Vagrant and another starter were grouped together in the betting field at the Kentucky Association track in Lexington. Vagrant didn't exactly bow out in a blaze of glory. He finished last.

He was through racing, but he didn't spend the rest of his life leisurely romping around a Bluegrass pasture. In his final days, he pulled a cart in Lexington.

Apollo (1882)

Apollo is the only Kentucky Derby winner who didn't race as a two-year-old. Making the first start of his career slightly more than a month before the 1882 Derby, he ran second in the mile-and-one-quarter Pickwick Stakes. Seven days later, in a race for all ages, he finished second in a pair of mile heats. Six days later, he captured the mile-and-a-half Cottrill Stakes. Those three races took place in New Orleans, and Apollo next appeared in competition in Louisville, where he won the Kentucky Derby in a stunning upset over the heralded Runnymede.

Runnymede, owned by the Dwyer Brothers (Mike and Phil), was pocketed at least twice in the Derby, then finally found clear sailing and took the lead in the upper stretch. The shout went up from the crowd that he would win, but perhaps overcoming his troubles in the race had taken too much out of him because he couldn't withstand Apollo's charge inside the furlong pole.

Runnymede's loss was a stunning upset, but the real thunderbolt came a few years later when a charge of scandal put a dark cloud over the 1882 Derby. Capt. S. S. Brown, a wealthy and prominent Pittsburgh horseman, contended that bookmakers had arranged for Runnymede to lose the Derby. With a large amount of money wagered on Runnymede in the winter books, a Derby victory by him would have ruined many bookies. Runnymede's loss meant that the bookmakers survived, and Brown's charge of foul play left the 1882 renewal tainted as the first Derby whose integrity was questioned.

Green Morris, co-owner and trainer of Apollo, was a formidable gambler who reportedly netted a cool ten thousand dollars in bets on the Derby victory. Morris was a good friend of the Dwyer Brothers and after the Derby assured the heavy-betting Mike Dwyer and others that the best horse had won. But six days after the Derby in the Clark Stakes, Runnymede simply outclassed Apollo, who finished third, ten to thirteen lengths behind the winner.

But it was Apollo's name, not Runnymede's, that went into the record books as the winner of the 1882 Derby, and afterward *The Kentucky Live Stock Record* provided this description of the victorious gelding: "He stands 15 hands half an inch high, and the only white is on the left hind pastern. He has a rather heavy, plain head, wide jowls, good stout neck, which fills up his shoulders well, mounts high on the withers, deep chest, good length, arched loin, long quarters and hips, with excellent, clean and bony legs."

Macbeth II (1888)

Macbeth II, bred by Rufus Lisle of Lexington, Kentucky, was out of a mare named Agnes, who also produced two third-place finishers in the Derby—Jacobin (1887) and Robespierre (1890). Years later, Joe Palmer wrote in *The Blood-Horse* magazine that Agnes was "a blind mare . . . which the Lisle family drove to a buggy between foals." George V. Hankins, nicknamed "The King of the Chicago Gamblers," purchased Macbeth II from Lisle in the fall of the gelding's two-year-old season. Racing for the Chicago Stable of Hankins and trainer John S. Campbell, Macbeth II wasn't particularly impressive on his way to the post for the 1888 Derby. "The one-time Derby favorite stepped sedately along, and his docility and rather languid movements elicited many repetitions of the often made assertion that he could not win, as he was too stale from over-work," declared *The Courier-Journal*.

But Macbeth II, under the handling of seventeen-year-old George Covington, did win, and the Chicago Stable reportedly cleaned up in bets (winter book or otherwise), different accounts putting the winnings at $25,000, $70,000 or $75,000.

Macbeth raced for seven seasons over an eight-year period, and his 106 starts ranked second among Derby winners to the 111 by Donau (1910).

One hundred years after Macbeth II's Derby victory, the knowledgeable Philip Von Borries looked back on the iron horse's career and wrote: "A decent stakes horse in his prime, he deteriorated into a claimer at the end, barely remembered by the turfwriters of his time. Subsequently lost to historians, Macbeth II endures today as one of the most anonymous winners ever in the history of the Derby."

Old Rosebud (1914)

Old Rosebud, owned by Hamilton C. "Ham" Applegate of Louisville, set a track record of 2:03 ^{2}/$_5$ in winning the

1914 Derby. Thanks chiefly to enterprising work of track superintendent Tom Young, the racing strip was in good enough condition for Old Rosebud to click off his blazing time. Days of rain had left the track a muddy mess, with numerous hoof prints filled with water. On the morning of the Derby, Young sent his crew of men to the track with sponges and buckets, and they proceeded to dry out every hole. By Derby post time, the track was listed as fast, and Old Rosebud toyed with his opponents in winning by at least eight lengths under a smooth ride by John McCabe.

"Old Rosebud was better than any of them," McCabe later said. "I mean better than Man o' War, Count Fleet, or Secretariat."

Said Applegate: "I've never seen anything I thought was as good as him, and I've seen an awful lot of horse races. He was very extraordinary."

Old Rosebud was just that. "Old Buddy" was recognized as the best racehorse in America in 1917, the year he won fifteen of twenty-one starts. He ran a total of seven seasons, including two starts each at ten and eleven years old. He is the only Derby winner in history to race at the age of eleven. Called "a prince of the turf," he captured forty of eighty races and took home $74,729 in purses, breaking the record of $71,875 set by 1881 Derby king Hindoo for most money earned by a Derby winner. In 1922, Old Rosebud suffered an ankle injury that necessitated his having to be destroyed. *The Thoroughbred Record* reported that Old Rosebud was shot at the Jamaica racetrack. The magazine reported that "the famous gelding stepped into a hole" in a May 17 race "and tore the ligaments of one ankle. It became evident that the horse would be a hopeless cripple. There were misty eyes at Jamaica when word went around that an old favorite had passed away. . . ."

Exterminator (1918)

Going off as the longest shot in the race at 29–1 odds, Exterminator won the Derby for owner Willis Sharpe Kilmer and went on to prove that this victory was no fluke. In a storied career that spanned eight years, he won fifty of one hundred races. A freight train on legs if there ever was one, he hauled more than six tons of weight—12,580½ pounds—in his career. In 1922, a year that he was the best racehorse in America, Exterminator averaged carrying 132.7 pounds per start (2,256 pounds for seventeen races). He packed the highest weight of his career in a 1922 race, finishing sixth with 140 pounds in the mile-and-a-half Independence Handicap at Latonia. That also was the year that he won with the most weight of his career—138 pounds in the mile-and-one-quarter Kentucky Handicap at Churchill Downs.

During his career, Exterminator raced a total of almost 125 miles in his one hundred starts.

"The people loved him," the esteemed Joe Estes wrote in *The Blood-Horse* magazine. "As he was somewhat angular in appearance, they called him Old Bones, or Old Slim. Despite the high weights he carried and the stiff competition he met, and despite the fact that he was kept in training two years beyond his 7-year-old prime, they made him favorite in 62 of the 98 starts in which there was betting—and collected their bets 38 times in the 62. They passed around among themselves the stories of him, not only of his class and courage, but of how smart he was, and what a good 'shipper.' He had become a folk-hero when he was finally retired from the tracks and pensioned."

David Alexander wrote of Exterminator: "He was an even-tempered horse and seemed almost human at times. At the post, if he were next to a fractious actor, he'd simply lean against him and hold him until the tape was sprung."

The beloved Exterminator lived to the age of thirty, dying of a heart attack on September 26, 1945. Col. Matt Winn, the guiding genius behind the Churchill Downs' success story, witnessed the first seventy-five runnings of the Derby and, as far as he was concerned, Exterminator was the best racehorse he ever saw. "He could do everything," Winn said.

Paul Jones (1920)

Paul Jones was bred in Kentucky by John E. Madden, the "Wizard of the Turf," and was bought on Ral Parr's behalf by trainer William "Uncle Billy" Garth at the Saratoga yearling sale. Following his purchase, the Parr stable decided to geld Paul Jones in the hope of changing his mean temper. Gelding him "brought a wonderful change in his habits," it was reported after the Derby, "but he is still none too gentle a thoroughbred."

Paul Jones could have been excused if he suffered from the Rodney Dangerfield complex at the 1920 Derby. The gelding didn't get much respect. Racing in an entry that went off at 16–1 odds, he was generally considered a second-stringer to Blazes, his stablemate who finished sixth.

Shortly before the Derby, one account called Paul Jones a colt (a mistake that appeared in print on more than this one occasion) and reported that he wasn't an impressive-looking horse. "No upstanding, commanding horse is he; rather a sedate and workmanlike sort, but horses do not run on looks and looks are chiefly a sales ring asset," the story said.

Beginning with the 1920 renewal, weights for the Derby have remained the same for each subsequent running—126 for colts and geldings, 121 for fillies. Had Paul Jones come along a year earlier for the 1919 Derby, he would have carried 119 pounds, the impost for geldings before the 1920 change.

Following his racing career, Paul Jones spent his retirement days as a qualified hunter in Virginia. For about the last half of his life, he was in the care of another owner, Mrs. John Porter Jones, daughter of Garth, the gelding's trainer. Her husband, well known as "Doc" Jones, was a physician who turned to training horses.

Mrs. Howard Y. Haffner, daughter of the Joneses, once recalled that Paul Jones "went lame and had to be nerved. They were going to destroy him or something."

Rather than have Paul Jones put down, Mrs. Jones asked for the horse, who was turned over to her.

"My father schooled him and rode him in pink coat races, gentleman races, and hunt races around," said Mrs. Haffner. "And then mother hunted him sidesaddle. She rode sidesaddle always. He was a family horse, really."

Mrs. Haffner used to ride Paul Jones herself. "I was young, but I rode him," she recalled. "He was quiet, a very gentle horse. A very smart, sensible horse. He was a brown horse with a white face and four white feet."

Paul Jones was destroyed at the age of thirteen due to physical infirmities. He was buried at the Inglecress Farm, Charlottesville, Virginia.

Clyde Van Dusen (1929)

Jockey Linus "Pony" McAtee had a blind date for the 1929 Derby. It was with Clyde Van Dusen, a horse the rider had never seen before he climbed aboard him for the Derby. Clyde Van Dusen was a small horse. So small that his trainer made a special trip to the jockeys' room before the Derby to tell McAtee not to let his heart sink or be discouraged over the horse's diminutiveness. "He can't be small enough to surprise me," McAtee assured the trainer, Clyde Van Dusen, for whom the horse was named. "I've ridden some mighty little horses."

Even though warned, McAtee was shocked when he arrived at the paddock and got his first glimpse of the gelding. "I was kinda scared when I first saw Clyde because he is so little," McAtee said after the gelding splattered home two lengths in front in the horse-and-buggy time of 2:10⁴/₅. "But now I can say he is one of the finest and gamest horses of them all. Oh, boy, how he can run! He is nothing but a mud-runnin' fool!"

Clyde Van Dusen wasn't the same horse later in his career that he was on Derby Day. He suffered an ignominious fall from glory. Once a stakes winner, he completed his career unable to even capture a claiming race.

There was a reason for the horse's decline, according to John Dishman, the man who raised Clyde Van Dusen. "Mr. Van was working him one day," the eighty-five-year-old Dishman recalled in 1979, "and he bit the pony Mr. Van was riding. And the old pony kicked him on the inside of his leg. It just swolled up on him, and he never did do no good after that."

Clyde Van Dusen won only once in 1930, and, after sitting out 1931 and 1932, he returned to action in 1933, running ten times, each a claiming race. He failed to win any of those ten.

In his final career start, he finished fourth, earning fifteen dollars—a far cry from the $53,950 he had picked up for his Derby victory.

Clyde Van Dusen subsequently was sent to Few Acres Farm, near Lexington, living a life of leisure. He grew heavier but stayed as frisky as ever. A companion of his in those days was an old pony named Bill or Pony Bill, the same lead pony who accompanied Clyde Van Dusen during his racing days.

After the old pony died, Clyde Van Dusen returned to the track—as a pony himself. The '29 Derby winner went back to the racetrack in California as Van Dusen's personal mount, leading the horses the trainer had in his string to the track in the mornings.

Apparently, no record was ever made of the death of Clyde Van Dusen. Like an old soldier, this little horse with the king-sized heart just faded away into obscurity.

7

Those Second-stringers Stand Tall

Where Was Chesapeake?

H. Price McGrath stood there wondering where Chesapeake, the prize three-year-old from his racing stable, was as the field for the first Kentucky Derby began to straighten out for home on that May afternoon in 1875. The highly regarded Chesapeake was back in the pack, far out of contention, as McGrath stood there apprehensively near the head of the stretch. But wait a minute. Who was that up there on the front end? Why, it was none other than Aristides, the "second-string" member of the McGrath entry.

Aristides? He had been entered as a rabbit—merely to set the pace for his more heralded stablemate, Chesapeake, yet he was still up there on the front end, still running his heart out. McGrath waved to Aristides' jockey, Oliver Lewis, to "go on," and the rider did just that, booting his mount home by a length.

Such was the story of Aristides as he overshadowed Chesapeake in the first Kentucky Derby. In the 117 subsequent runnings of America's most famous horse race, similar stories have unfolded in which the "second-stringer" has outrun or successfully filled in for a more publicized or higher-valued stablemate.

Owners, as well as trainers and jockeys, occasionally have underestimated the abilities of the lesser-known horses in their camps. And sometimes turf writers—yes, even those omniscient turf writers—have been made to look like dopes, instead of dopesters, when it comes to rating horses from the same stable.

Where Was Sun Briar?

He was back in the barn, probably reading his scrapbook, as his "ugly duckling" stablemate, Exterminator, went off as the longest price on the board in the 1918 Derby.

Sun Briar was treated as something special by his owner, Willis Sharpe Kilmer. After all, how many horses do you know who have birthday parties? Sun Briar had one—cake and all the trimmings—on January 1, 1918, at Kilmer's estate in Binghamton, New York.

As a standout juvenile in 1917, Sun Briar had won $59,505, more than any other horse in America had earned that year. But in a prep race at Lexington less than three weeks before the Derby, he looked far from sharp in finishing third. Kilmer, thinking that his star needed more training under simulated race conditions, acquired a three-year-old gelding, Exterminator, to serve as a trial horse for Sun Briar.

To a few railbirds, Exterminator looked more like a Derby horse than Sun Briar did in their workouts. But not to Kilmer. "I do not consider Exterminator in the same class with Sun Briar," the owner insisted.

On Derby Day, though, Sun Briar was confined to the barn. He wasn't right and hadn't trained satisfactorily in his most recent works. With Sun Briar out, according to one story, Kilmer originally had intended to ship his horses to New York, but when a transportation mix-up delayed his stable's departure from Churchill Downs, the owner decided to go ahead and enter Exterminator in the Derby.

Everyone knows the rest of the story. Exterminator, the pinch runner, confounded the experts by winning the Derby at a $61.20 straight payoff. His trainer, Henry McDaniel, admitted that he hadn't bet the first nickel on the horse. And his jockey, Willie Knapp, maintained that Sun Briar was still the superior runner. "I always thought that I'd ride the Derby winner," Knapp said, "but I never dreamed Exterminator would be my mount. I had counted on riding Sun Briar, and had that colt started he would have won the race without question."

Said Kilmer: "Exterminator sure is a great horse—and he can have anything he wants in Binghamton." All Exterminator wanted was to run and run and run. "Old Bones," as he came to be known, started a whopping one hundred times in his illustrious career, winning exactly half of those races.

Where Was Billy Kelly?

He was running second at the finish of the 1919 Derby, five full lengths behind his supposedly inferior stablemate, Sir Barton. But even in defeat, Billy Kelly accounted for a higher financial return for his owner, Comdr. J. K. L. Ross, than did Sir Barton.

Sir Barton, who ran for co-breeder John E. Madden in his first four starts before being purchased by Ross as a juvenile, was a maiden (0 for 6) entering the Derby. But he ended his drought on Derby Day, a triumph that was worth $20,825 to Ross. Billy Kelly, meanwhile, earned twenty-five hundred dollars in purse money for finishing second but, moreover, netted Ross a cool fifty thousand for beating his rival, Eternal.

It seems that several months before the race, Ross and Arnold Rothstein, a notorious gambler, had made a horse-and-horse bet on the 1919 Derby. Ross took Billy Kelly and Rothstein had Eternal. The amount of the bet was fifty thousand dollars, with the stipulation that in order for either man to win, his horse had to post an in-the-money finish.

As for Sir Barton, according to one newspaper account, he wasn't even considered a good bet to run in the Derby just a day before the race. Without elaborating, a story on the eve of the big race stated that "Sir Barton may not run in the Derby."

Sir Barton ran in the Derby, to be sure. He ran like he had never run before, leading from start to finish in a genuine surprise. Billy Kelly, although soundly whipped by Sir Barton, didn't embarrass himself with his second-place finish. But Eternal, who went off as a favorite with stablemate Sailor, finished a dismal tenth, 28½ lengths behind Sir Barton.

Sir Barton went on to prove that his Derby success was very much for real. The Ross colt subsequently captured the Preakness and Belmont Stakes to become the first horse in American racing history to win the Triple Crown.

As it turned out, the Derby was one of only four times that Sir Barton outran Billy Kelly in their twelve career meetings. Billy Kelly finished ahead of Sir Barton all three times that they met in 1918, once in 1919, and in each of their four encounters in 1920. Billy Kelly won six of the eight starts in which he finished ahead of Sir Barton. Billy Kelly's advantage in the eight races was fifty-six lengths.

Meanwhile, Sir Barton came in ahead of Billy Kelly by sixteen and a half lengths the four times that he whipped his stablemate, all in 1919—the Kentucky Derby, the Potomac Handicap, the Pimlico Fall Serial Weight-For-Age Races No. 2 and 3.

Even though he finished behind Billy Kelly two-thirds of the times that they met, Sir Barton won the one that counted the most—that 1919 Derby, a race that served as a launching pad to his sweep of the Triple Crown.

Where in Blazes Were Blazes, Donnacona, Wildair, and Damask?

They were all out of the money in the 1920 Derby, but not to worry. Their lesser-regarded stablemates came through, finishing 1-2-3.

First of all, there was Blazes, who finished sixth while stablemate Paul Jones won the Derby.

Paul Jones generally wasn't rated the better half of the entry. After the Derby, he was described by one newspaper as "despised and ignored, the 'weak sister' of his stable." Another publication referred to him as "the ugly little brown."

Ral Parr, the Baltimore man in whose name the entry raced, said afterward: "I always had a lot of confidence in Paul Jones and the way that he trained for the race made me real sweet on his chances to win the big stake. Naturally, I thought that Blazes, my other horse, was the best, but in my mind there was not a whole lot of difference between them. When I saw Paul Jones go to the front right at the outset, I knew that it was going to be a tough job to catch him—and so it proved. I'll never forget the thrill as my colors came down in front. I guess Paul Jones is a better horse than we thought."

In handicapping the coming three-year-olds of 1920, C. C. Ridley of *Daily Racing Form* tabbed Man o' War at 136 pounds and Blazes was next at 120. Trainer William Garth started off the year with high Derby hopes for Blazes. A month before the big race, *The Thoroughbred Record* magazine reported: "William Garth . . . recently declared in the East that he was ready to back Blazes at even money, play or pay, against any three-year-old entered in the Kentucky Derby. The long-legged, short-bodied son of Wrack-Blazing Star was more than a good two-year-old last year, but he had a pretty stiff campaign. He is said to have wintered unusually well and to be as lusty as a bear."

However, on Derby Day, *The Louisville Times* stated that Garth liked Paul Jones' chances better than he did those of Blazes. "Paul Jones and Blazes have outside chances, especially if the track is muddy," the paper said. "The first named has been working better than Blazes, and is better fancied by trainer Billy Garth, who says both are fit and ready to run."

Donnacona was picked to win the Derby on all three lists of selections appearing in *The Courier-Journal*. Paul Jones wasn't mentioned among the first three in any of their predictions.

The Louisville Times ran seven selections, and the best mention for Paul Jones was a single third-place finish. Picked to win in the *Times'* list of selections were Wildair by two experts, Donnacona by one, the Harry Payne Whitney entry by three others, and Upset by the *Racing Form*.

Paul Jones won the Derby by a head over Upset, with On Watch third. The result came as quite a surprise. As one article noted after the Derby, the prophets fell flat on their faces. "The three horses that finished in the money were passed over by the alleged turf experts who gave vent to their opinions," the story said. "And they were not alone in their misguided predictions. Owners and trainers of the fortunate trio discounted their ability. Trainer Billy Garth of the Parr stable considered Blazes the better of his pair; Trainer Jimmy Rowe banked on Wildair and Damask; Trainer Max Hirsch declared Donnacona worth two of On Watch."

Upset clearly hadn't been given as much chance as his stablemates. A story appearing two days before the 1920 Derby said that "Wildair and Damask will be the chief dependence of the Harry Payne Whitney stable." The story added: "Upset also will sport silks in the big race, although he is not considered as formidable as his companions." (Interestingly, though considered no better than a third-stringer in his stable at the time of the Derby, Upset had earned his place in racing history the year before by beating Man o' War, a feat no other horse ever accomplished.)

Damask came in fourth, trailing Upset by eight lengths. Wildair was eighth, almost fifteen lengths behind Upset. Donnacona was fifth, six lengths behind On Watch. As for Blazes, he finished fourteen lengths behind Paul Jones in the Derby. "Paul Jones' victory saved the makers of future books thousands," wrote Vernon Sanders of *The Louisville Times*. Where Blazes was among those horses well-backed in the future books, Sanders noted, "It is doubtful if the future bookmakers wrote Paul Jones' name. So there you are—it's hard to pick the winners."

Where Was Black Servant?

He was just where he was expected to be—on the lead— as the field thundered down the stretch for the finish of the 1921 Kentucky Derby. Funny thing, though. Black Servant didn't keep the lead.

Well, it wasn't so funny to certain bettors, particularly those folks from Idle Hour Farm who couldn't believe their eyes when Behave Yourself—a stablemate, of all things—came on to beat Black Servant by a head for the roses.

The two Idle Hour horses ran against each other in five races during their careers, all in 1920, and the Derby was the only time that Behave Yourself finished ahead of Black Servant. In three of the races that Black Servant outran Behave Yourself, the difference between the two was twenty and three-fourths lengths. In their other meeting, Black Servant ran second and Behave Yourself broke down.

Col. E. R. Bradley, the owner of Idle Hour, had a high opinion of Black Servant. Leading up to the Derby, one story reported that Colonel Bradley "is said to have made the statement that he considered Black Servant twenty pounds better than any horse he has ever owned."

According to legend, Colonel Bradley stood to make more than $250,000 in the winter books if Black Servant won the Derby. But Olin Gentry, who was employed by Bradley at Idle Hour for twenty-five years, maintained that the tale of the colonel's winter-book bet on Black Servant was nothing more than a fairy tale.

"There isn't a word of truth to that," Gentry said. "Of course, Mr. Bradley wanted Black Servant to win because he owned his sire, Black Toney, and he didn't own the sire of Behave Yourself."

Even if Bradley didn't wager on Black Servant, as Gentry maintained, others at the Lexington, Kentucky, farm did. Gentry noted that "everybody on the farm wanted to kill" Charles Thompson, who gave Behave Yourself a rousing ride to win the Derby.

"The people on the farm and Mr. Bradley's friends and all had bet on Black Servant in the winter book, and when they got beat, they did a lot of talking, and people just got to figuring that if all the people on the farm lost their money on Black Servant, then Mr. Bradley did, too. But he told me that he didn't bet a dime on Black Servant in the winter book."

Where Was Sun Beau?

To Willis Sharpe Kilmer's dismay, he was finishing back in the ruck—eleventh place, to be exact—in the 1928 Derby, while onetime stablemate Reigh Count was rolling home on top.

Kilmer sometimes had trouble recognizing potential in a horse. Remember, this was the same man who lucked into winning the 1918 Derby by starting Exterminator as a pinch runner. With fate having given him a Derby winner

All eight feet were off the ground as stablemates Exterminator (left) and Sun Briar worked out at Saratoga after the 1918 Kentucky Derby. As a pinch runner for Sun Briar, longshot Exterminator captured the 1918 Derby and paid $61.20 to win. (Courtesy Keeneland-Cook)

in 1918, Kilmer had no complaints coming about parting with Reigh Count, whom he had bred. Kilmer, who twice was to head the American standings for victories by a breeder (1939 and 1941), ran his thoroughbred operation in such a way that his horses were for sale at almost any time, provided that the price was right. Sun Beau, whom he also bred, reportedly was available for eight hundred dollars at one time but was never sold.

Reigh Count had shown Kilmer nothing early in his two-year-old season. But John D. Hertz had seen something—a fighting instinct—that impressed him about the colt. Hertz, the Yellow Cab magnate, liked what he saw when he watched Reigh Count reach over and bite at a horse's neck in a race at Saratoga. "I like that colt," Hertz said to a companion in the stands. "He's a fighter, and I admire any kind of a fighter. I'd like to buy him."

Hertz, a former boxer, later bought Reigh Count for $12,500 after the colt had scored his first victory in seven starts. For the rest of 1927, Reigh Count won three of seven races for his new stable and gained acclaim with Dice as the finest two-year-old colts in the land.

Selling Reigh Count, of course, was a mistake. Kilmer, though, could be a hard man to convince. He claimed that Sun Beau was the finest horse he ever bred. To Kilmer's chagrin, Sun Beau was never able to beat Reigh Count in three meetings. Reigh Count, who proved to be the country's best three-year-old colt of 1928, finished ahead of Sun Beau by a total of almost thirty lengths in those three races, including a difference of nineteen lengths in the Derby.

Tedd H. Kline of *The Cleveland News* wrote after that the Churchill Downs classic: "The Derby winner is a cast-off. Yep, it's true. Willie Sharpe Kilmer, the Binghamton, N.Y., sportsman, sold him to the Hertz family last year because he thought that either Sun Edwin or Sun Beau was a better colt, and would win more races for him in 3-year-old form. . . . Had (Kilmer's) foresight been good last year, Reigh Count would have scored in his colors today."

Where Was Brother Joe?

Oh, brother! Would you believe that this Idle Hour Farm horse, once considered a better prospect than Burgoo King, came in nineteenth in the 1932 Derby? Burgoo King won the Derby, finishing forty-five lengths ahead of his brother from Idle Hour Farm.

Actually, Brother Joe wasn't a brother to Burgoo King. Rather, he was closely related to Blue Larkspur, the best horse ever to race for Col. E. R. Bradley. Both had the same dam, Blossom Time. Brother Joe was by Black Toney, the father of Blue Larkspur's sire, Black Servant.

Olin Gentry, the longtime employee of Colonel Bradley, once said of Brother Joe: "He went into winter quarters as the best prospect because he could run and he was a brother to Blue Larkspur. But Brother Joe went lame. He had a bad leg. I think he went in there with a half-bowed tendon. I don't know why in the hell they ran him. But anyhow we just thought Burgoo King was the best before the Derby 'cause the other horse wasn't sound."

Brother Joe, whose troublesome leg began to bother him going down the backstretch, was eased near the end of the Derby and was gimpy afterward. He was incapacitated for the rest of 1932. This bad-legged colt couldn't have beaten Broadway Joe, bad knees and all, in the Derby.

One story indicated that the Derby loss didn't detract from Bradley's opinion of Brother Joe. After the colt was injured in the Derby and finished ahead of only a horse that had broken down, *The Courier-Journal* reported, "Mr. Bradley contended all along that Brother Joe was the better colt of the two and he has not weakened on him yet, as his race in the Derby does not count."

Where Was Devil Diver?

Eddie Arcaro knew where Devil Diver was. Arcaro also knew where he could have been sitting on that afternoon at Churchill Downs. On Shut Out's back, of course.

Arcaro had the choice of riding Devil Diver or Shut Out.

Given the choice between riding those two Greentree Stable colts, which one would *you* have taken? Devil Diver had finished ahead of Shut Out in four of five previous meetings but had missed some preparation due to an injury suffered at Keeneland. Tough choice, right? Well, Arcaro had to make such a decision, and he picked Devil Diver, who came home sixth in the Derby, about seven and a half lengths behind Shut Out.

Arcaro, who rode five Derby winners in his career, wasn't exactly in a rosy mood after the 1942 renewal. "I feel bad enough," the chagrined rider snapped as he jerked off a boot in the jockeys' quarters. "Why ask me any questions? Dammit, you saw the race. I just made a mistake."

Arcaro wasn't the only one who made a mistake. In a poll of twenty-three turf writers, eight picked Devil Diver to win. Not one named Shut Out.

The Greentree stablemates both ran in the Preakness, Shut Out finishing fifth and Devil Diver eighth. They met five other times in their careers, and Devil Diver came in ahead of Shut Out in each race, including victories in the Toboggan, Metropolitan, and Brooklyn handicaps of 1943 and the Toboggan Handicap of 1944. Devil Diver, who thus held a 9–3 advantage over Shut Out, was a champion handicap runner at four and five and later was inducted into racing's Hall of Fame. Shut Out was neither a champion nor a Hall of Famer. But he beat Devil Diver on the first Saturday in May of 1942, a day that Eddie Arcaro will never forget.

Where Was De Luxe?

He wasn't where his stablemate, Ponder, was the first time the field of fourteen passed the finish line in the 1949 Derby. Ponder was a plodding last. De Luxe wasn't where Ponder was at the finish either. Ponder was a flying first.

Lest you get the wrong impression, it should be noted that De Luxe didn't get a chance to run in the Derby. It's a good thing, too. He might still be trying to finish the race.

Ben A. Jones, who trained the two horses for Calumet Farm, considered De Luxe the better colt. But in prepping for the Derby in the six-and-a-half-furlong Glenview Purse at Keeneland, Ponder finished fourth and De Luxe brought up the rear in the six-horse field, some thirteen and a half lengths behind his stablemate. Jones immediately charged that somebody must have tampered with De Luxe.

"I'll never understand how he was beaten a dozen lengths by Ponder," Jones declared. "Why, he always has been a dozen lengths better than Ponder."

Earl Ruby, sports editor of *The Courier-Journal*, asked Mike Barry of the *Kentucky Irish American* if he thought there was anything to Jones' charge. "Forget it," Barry told Ruby. "Ben's been too high on De Luxe all along. He didn't beat Ponder because he didn't figure to beat Ponder."

Barry was right. Ponder figured to beat the overrated De Luxe.

In the Derby Trial, Ponder finished second to Olympia, and De Luxe was dead last, fourteen lengths behind the winner.

The unsung Ponder went on to win the Derby at a thirty-four-dollar mutuel. According to Jerry McNerney of *The Courier-Journal*, the victory caused Jones to pinch himself "in utter disbelief . . . and not until they hung up the numbers did he seem to believe what he had just seen."

What Jones saw was Ponder burst from nowhere to win by three lengths in a stunning upset.

" . . . Ponder was the horse that Jones and all Calumet Farm said was nothing only three weeks ago," McNerney wrote in his Derby account. "And Ponder was the horse they said couldn't run in the same racing league with the start of their stable—De Luxe. And Ponder was the horse that even Jones said yesterday was just running for a piece of the money. 'Nothing in the race will be able to come close to Olympia,' Jones had predicted."

Olympia wound up sixth as the odds-on favorite.

Not only did Ponder win the Derby, but when he retired from racing, he had a record of eleven stakes victories and $541,275 in earnings. De Luxe won two stakes and $56,785 in his racing career.

Is there any reason to ponder which of these horses indeed was deluxe?

Where Was Air Lift?

Sadly, he was dead, having to be destroyed after suffering a compound fracture of an ankle in his first start on July 27, 1949, at Jamaica. The full brother to 1946 Triple Crown champion Assault was considered the best colt in King Ranch's crop of 1947 foals. Middleground was among the horses in that crop, and his name was proof positive that his stable was on middle ground in trying to determine what kind of future he had.

As his owner, Robert J. Kleberg, once recalled: " . . . early in his two-year-old year I was inspecting all the two-year-olds and at that particular time I used to send some of them to California and part of them to New York, the best usually going to New York. Middleground had not been named, and I personally led him out of the stall. I was so impressed by his disposition and, for that matter, his breeding and appearance that I made the remark, 'I'm on middle ground as far as this colt is concerned, whether to send him east or west.' He was sent east. The rest is history."

In retrospect, maybe he should have been named Hallowed Ground. After all, that's what he stood on in the charmed infield winner's circle at Churchill Downs on May 6, 1950.

Where Was Gen. Duke?

The Calumet Farm's winter-book favorite was on the sidelines, scratched the morning of the 1957 Derby because of a foot injury. (It later was discovered that he had a fracture of his left front foot.)

Gen. Duke and Iron Liege, both sons of Bull Lea, had gone to the post in the same race eight times. The advantage easily belonged to Gen. Duke, who finished ahead of Iron Liege on six of those occasions. The margins between the two in the eight races were in Gen. Duke's favor by fifteen and a half lengths.

But he couldn't make it to the post for the Derby. Iron Liege, described as a "buck private" in Calumet's Derby plans, was still around, but he wasn't a horse of Gen. Duke's caliber. Even so, he was still good enough on Derby Day to win out over such standout opponents as Gallant Man, Round Table, and Bold Ruler in a field called by many the greatest in the race's history.

Where Was Tuleg?

On the afternoon of May 2, 1959, he was in a stall, munching on hay and perhaps thinking back to a plane trip he had made from England a couple of years earlier. Texas oilman and rancher Fred W. Turner Jr., represented by bloodstock agent Bert Kerr, bought Tuleg as a youngster for twenty-five thousand dollars at the Newmarket sales. Turner also instructed Kerr to buy another horse primarily to keep Tuleg company on the flight across the Atlantic. That horse was purchased for a modest $6,762.

On Derby Day '59, the traveling companion—a colt who answered to the name of Tomy Lee—picked up $119,650 by winning the Run for the Roses. As things turned out, Tuleg had run his final race on April 15, 1959, at Keeneland, finishing last in an allowance. His career totals: ten starts, one win, three seconds, and one third with earnings of $17,250. Tomy Lee rolled up earnings of $405,014 with a record of fourteen wins, four seconds, and three thirds in thirty-one starts. Not bad for a traveling companion.

Where Was Bold Lad?

He was taking his good old time circling the Downs track. Dapper Dan, meanwhile, was running out of time as he missed by a neck catching Lucky Debonair in the 1965 Derby.

Bold Lad, the two-year-old champion of 1964, was sent off as the Derby's 2–1 favorite. Dapper Dan was a 30–1 outsider. Although both were trained by Bill Winfrey, they ran as separate betting interests because they were the property of different owners. Bold Lad represented the Wheatley Stable, and Dapper Dan was owned by Ogden Phipps.

"Oh, Dapper Dan will go a mile and a quarter," Winfrey told a group of reporters a couple of days before the race. "It's just a matter of how long it'll take him."

Winfrey's comment drew some hearty laughs from the gentlemen of the Fourth Estate, only one of whom went out on a limb in a poll of 122 writers to pick Dapper Dan to win the 1965 Derby. Thirty-four selected Bold Lad. For the record, it took Dapper Dan two minutes, one and one-fifth seconds to run the Derby's mile and a quarter. His clocking for the final half-mile was a sizzling forty-seven seconds flat.

It's unfortunate that nobody had a stopwatch on Winfrey to see if he set any speed records getting out of town with Bold Lad, who finished next to last.

Where Was Cup Race?

Like his half-brother Graustark, Cup Race was forced to miss the Derby due to an injury. Graustark was the ill-fated Darby Dan Farm colt who was hailed by many as a potential super horse before a broken coffin bone suffered in the Blue Grass Stakes ended his racing career prior to the 1966 Derby.

At the start of the 1967 season, Cup Race was rated Darby Dan's chief contender for the three-year-old classics. In appraising Cup Race before the colt's first career start in 1967, Darby Dan trainer Loyd "Boo" Gentry said: "All I know is that he does everything like a good horse. I don't expect another Graustark, but I have to think he's a real runner."

Cup Race then went out and won his career debut by seven lengths at Hialeah Park, running six furlongs in 1:10³/₅. "Real happy," Gentry said afterward. "Ran just like we hoped he would, the way we expected he would."

A week later at Hialeah, Cup Race won again, but this time by just three-quarters of a length in 1:11²/₅ for six furlongs. He came out of this allowance race with bucked shins. So much for his Derby plans.

Proud Clarion, meanwhile, was still winless at this stage of the proceedings. He was 0 for 3 as a juvenile before breaking his maiden in his three-year-old unveiling, an eight-length score at Hialeah on February 8, 1967, just three months before the Kentucky Derby. "He was a kind of horse you like, then you don't like," Gentry later said of

Proud Clarion. "Delicate, nervous, bucked his shins, had a little ring bone, just couldn't get excited about him, you know, as a two-year-old. He wasn't like Cup Race, who just does everything right."

For the record, Cup Race—the colt who did "everything right"—started in eight races in his career (never in a stakes), won four times, and earned all of $20,500. As for Proud Clarion, he came into the Derby having run in only one stakes, a second-place finish in the Blue Grass. Nobody compared him to Graustark and relatively few bettors called out his number at the mutuel windows, but Proud Clarion burst from obscurity to win the Derby at a $62.20 payoff.

As for the "experts," they were really sharp on this second-stringer. Whereas they all had missed on Shut Out and only one had gone with Dapper Dan in 1965, a grand total of five writers picked Proud Clarion in 1967.

Five out of 111, that is.

Where Was Judger?

He was getting caught in more jams than a motorist does in rush-hour traffic on a Los Angeles freeway. A come-from-behind horse such as Judger found it impossible to weave his way through the traffic in the Kentucky Derby's one hundredth running, which attracted a record twenty-three starters in 1974.

Judger drew the No. 22 post position, and the best he could do was an eighth-place finish.

Owned by Seth Hancock, Judger ran in an entry (favored at 3–2) with Cannonade, who represented John M. Olin. Both colts, who were trained by W. C. "Woody" Stephens, had run against each other in three races leading into the Derby, and each time Judger finished ahead of Cannonade—by a total of fourteen and a half lengths. In one of their meetings, the Florida Derby, Judger won by three-quarters of a length over runner-up Cannonade. "Cannonade probably should have beat Judger in the Florida Derby," Stephens recalled. "Pete Anderson, I thought, moved too quick on Cannonade that day."

Judger generally was considered to be the better of the two colts. He was the program selection to win the Derby, and, in a poll of a hundred or so writers, he was the pick of 40 percent of them. Rube the Great was the second choice, while Cannonade received "scattered support," it was reported.

Interestingly, however, in the "Experts' Selections" column in the *Daily Racing Form*, Judger and Cannonade were the consensus co-picks, each receiving fourteen points. In those selections, Judger was Sweep's best bet of the day and was also the choice of Hermis. The clocker and trackman Bud Lyon each picked Cannonade to win.

Several years later, Red Smith wrote that "Stephens has said that contrary to the popular notion, he had a sneaking suspicion that Cannonade was the better runner."

Both colts were coming into the Derby off solid victories, Judger rallying for a four-length score in the Blue Grass Stakes at Keeneland and Cannonade winning the seven-furlong Stepping Stone Purse at Churchill Downs a week before the Derby. "Getting a race over the track with Cannonade opening day at Louisville might have made me win the Derby," Stephens said. "And post position, too. Judger had 22, and he was eliminated."

Stephens also pointed out that Flip Sal broke down in front of Judger—"and that cost him his chances going down the backside."

Cannonade, under a superb ride from Angel Cordero Jr., won, finishing eight lengths ahead of Judger. "I've never seen a better-rode race than Cordero rode on Cannonade that day," Stephens said.

A bet on the Judger-Cannonade entry at Churchill Downs paid five dollars to win. Cannonade, however, didn't receive that kind of support in the Off-Track Betting Corp.'s wagering in New York. He paid $18.80 to win in the OTB.

Cannonade never did win again, though. Judger didn't enjoy a better fate himself after the Derby. He started only one more time—and that, too, was a loss, a fifth-place finish in the Jersey Derby.

Where Were Chumming and Highland Park?

They were finishing behind their stablemates in the 1983 Derby. Not only that, but neither of them ran again. (For that matter, neither did one of the stablemates.)

Chumming ran in an entry with Caveat. The two colts had different owners, but both were trained by Woody Stephens. In the Experimental Free Handicap, Caveat and Chumming were rated at 119 and 115 pounds, respectively. But when the first future-book odds came out for the 1983 Derby, Chumming was a shorter price (15–1) than Caveat (20–1). Moreover, in the April 13, 1983, issue of *The Thoroughbred Record*, a poll of the magazine's correspondents had Chumming ranked third in the Derby ratings, while Caveat wasn't in the top ten.

By the time the first Saturday in May rolled around, Caveat was picked to finish third by Hermis and Sweep in the "Experts' Selections" column appearing in *Daily Racing Form*'s Derby Day edition. Chumming wasn't mentioned in the top three of any of the selections.

These two colts met twice before the Derby. In the Florida Derby, Chumming was fifth and Caveat tenth. And then in the Derby Trial, Caveat won and Chumming ran fifth.

Chumming sold for $1 million as a yearling, and when he went to the post in the '83 Derby, he became the race's first starter who ever sold for seven figures as a yearling.

He made history in that respect, but not in the way he ran. Chumming came in twelfth, some nine lengths behind third-place Caveat.

Chumming injured a coffin bone in the Derby, suffering a hairline fracture that was slow to heal, and he was retired.

Entrymates Highland Park and Freezing Rain never raced again either after the '83 Derby.

Freezing Rain lived in the shadow of stablemate Highland Park. Highland Park, whose Experimental Free Handicap assignment of 121 ranked below only three colts on the list, opened the Derby's future book as the 6–1 third choice, and Freezing Rain was 50–1. Highland Park entered the Derby with victories in five stakes and a bankroll of $382,858. Freezing Rain, meanwhile, had won two stakes and put together earnings of $89,325.

Highland Park had more impressive credentials than his stablemate, but he had been very ill earlier in the year and he never should have run in the Derby. In the Blue Grass Stakes, the only time the two stablemates met before the Derby, Freezing Rain finished fifth, five and one-quarter lengths in front of seventh-place Highland Park. In the Derby, Freezing Rain came in thirteenth, seven lengths in front of Highland Park, who was seventeenth.

Where Were Devil's Bag, Althea, and Vanlandingham?

Devil's Bag, the heralded champion two-year-old colt of 1983, was back in his stall at Churchill Downs, while Althea and Vanlandingham were finishing behind entrymates in the 1984 Run for the Roses.

Just as Woody Stephens had won the '74 Derby with a horse (Cannonade) who generally wasn't considered the equal of another in the trainer's stable (Judger), the Hall of Fame horseman came along ten years later to grab the roses with Swale, who had to take a back seat to Devil's Bag when it came to receiving rave notices.

Interestingly, on March 1, 1984, at Hialeah Park, Stephens pointed to Swale in his stall and said, "He's the horse that might win the Derby. He'll get the distance—and he's tough."

Stephens was right: Swale did get the Derby distance, winning by three and a fourth lengths. Devil's Bag, who sat out the Derby, was retired two days later, an announcement coming out that a veterinarian's examination revealed a small fracture of the radial carpal bone in his right knee.

Then there were Althea and Life's Magic, two fillies trained by D. Wayne Lukas. The entry went off as the favorite in the '84 Derby. Althea was considered the stronger half of the entry and was the program selection, but she wound up nineteenth after leading in the early going. Life's Magic finished eighth, twenty-two and a half lengths ahead of Althea.

Althea entered the Kentucky Derby off a seven-length Arkansas Derby victory in track-record time for the mile and one-eighth. She ran a tremendous race in winning the Arkansas Derby, but the big one came on the first Saturday in May at Churchill Downs and Althea didn't turn in a repeat performance. "It's hard for those fillies to put two *giant* races back to back against the colts," Lukas said, "and she certainly put one in in Arkansas."

Lukas added that Life's Magic "just came up" to the Kentucky Derby "a little better."

The 1984 renewal marked the only time that two fillies have run as an entry in the Derby. Both were champions— Althea doing her thing in 1983 as the champion two-year-old filly, and Life's Magic going on in 1984 to win the Eclipse Award as best three-year-old filly and in 1985 as best older female.

And then there was the Loblolly Stable entry of Vanlandingham and Pine Circle, both sons of Cox's Ridge. Vanlandingham came into the Derby victorious in all but one of his five starts, while Pine Circle entered the big race having won only one of his ten outings, even though he had earned more money than his stablemate ($146,935 to $106,560).

So Pine Circle went out there and finished sixth, almost twelve lengths in front of Vanlandingham in sixteenth place.

"It would be less than honest to say that I was paying much attention to Pine Circle during the race as we all felt that Vanlandingham was a better colt and Pine Circle comes from so far back," Loblolly owner John Ed Anthony recalled later that year.

Vanlandingham suffered a small fracture in his right front pastern in the Derby and didn't race again that year. However, he came back as a four-year-old and won the Eclipse Award as champion older horse.

Plain Ben Jones, trainer of a record six Kentucky Derby winners.
(Courtesy Keeneland Library, Lexington, Kentucky)

8

Plain Ben: The Greatest of All Derby Trainers

WHEN BEN A. JONES LOOKED at a horse, he could see more in a matter of minutes than some trainers could in months of observation. But Jones—or Plain Ben, as he was called—had more than an eye for a horse. He had an ear, too, as trainer Harvey Vanier pointed out in a story he remembered about Jones.

"Ben was my friend, and he was also my idol," said Vanier. "Ben was just great. I've been around many good horsemen, but he was one of the best. We were sitting in the tack room one time at Keeneland, and I was talking to him. We were having some coffee. Couldn't see the shed, but his horses were walking around the barn. The shedrow was kinda hard, and you could hear their feet hitting the ground as they walked over it."

Jones could hear that one of the horses wasn't hitting the ground as hard with one foot as he should have been, recalled Vanier. "He yelled out there to the shed and said, 'How long's that horse been walking lame in that right front?' I got up and looked out. Sure enough, he was walking off in his right front leg. I always wondered how B. A., not even knowing the horse, could tell which leg that horse was walking off in. He could tell the way he was stepping lightly over the ground. That's indicative of what a good horseman he was."

A good horseman, indeed. He was enshrined in racing's

Hall of Fame in 1958, he trained a record six Kentucky
Derby winners, and he conditioned nine champions.
Moreover, he was the country's leading trainer in money
won four years (1941, 1943, 1944, and 1952).

Eddie Arcaro referred to Jones as "the greatest trainer I
ever rode for. Ben did things with a horse that other
trainers will be copying for years."

Calumet Farm owner Warren Wright Sr. referred to
Jones as "the best horse in my barn."

Born in 1882 outside Parnell, Missouri, Benjamin Allyn
Jones grew up on his father's cattle farm. "When I was a
boy," he once drawled, "I was crazy about horses and Hol-
stein cows. Couldn't decide which I liked better. When I
got big enough to help with the milking, I made up my
mind."

Jones considered Kentucky his second home. He made a
big part of his reputation, as well as countless friends, in
the Bluegrass State. As Jerry McNerney of *The Courier-
Journal* once wrote, "He lived from one Derby to the next.
Winning it or losing it, he always started planning for the
next one the day after a Derby was run.

"Success and security didn't change him," McNerney
wrote. "Although he sported a big white hat, it didn't cover
a big head. Ben Jones remained 'Plain Ben'—friendly,
agreeable and always a hard worker. He knew that when
you got on top, you couldn't sit still; you had to work twice
as hard to stay there."

Plain Ben ran his first Derby starter in 1938, coming to
Louisville with Lawrin who had missed a lot of training
due to foot trouble. Away from competition since his
length-and-a-half victory in the Flamingo in late February,
Lawrin returned to action more than two months later,
finishing third in the six-furlong Daniel Boone Purse,
which was run on April 30, opening day of the Churchill
Downs spring meeting. Three days later, Lawrin ran

second in the one-mile Derby Trial, losing by a head to The Chief, who equaled the track record of 1:35⁴/₅.

Jones had Lawrin reshod for the Derby, removing the bar shoes that had been used for protection. "If he can run that good with those big heavy shoes on, he'll be ten pounds better when they're taken off," Jones said.

The heavy shoes were replaced with lightweight plates, and Lawrin proceeded to win the Derby by a length under Arcaro.

On September 1, 1939, Jones went to work as Calumet's trainer, and with Plain Ben running the show, the stable developed into a dynasty.

The first Calumet horse Jones ran in the Derby was Whirlaway in 1941. Whirlaway was a temperamental colt, one given to running to the outside rail in his races. He bore out in two preps leading up to the Derby, losing both times under young jockey Wendell Eads. Jones then summoned Arcaro to ride Whirlaway in the Derby.

The patient Jones, determined to teach Whirlaway to run a straight course, devised a special one-eyed blinker for the horse, giving him unobstructed vision with his left eye. Jones then called for a four-furlong test the day before the race. Sitting on a stable pony several feet out from the rail, Jones directed Arcaro to ride Whirlaway through the narrow opening. "I said to myself, if the old man is game enough to stand right there, I'm game enough to run him down," Arcaro remarked.

Whirlaway ran right through the opening, and with the lesson learned, he outclassed the field in the Derby, winning in a track-record 2:01²/₅, and went on to carry the Calumet devil's red and blue silks to a Triple Crown sweep.

Jones won his third Derby in 1944 with Pensive, a 7–1 shot. "Pensive was a runner, but he had bad feet," Jones recalled. "There were times when he could beat anyone. Yet, I was awfully lucky with him. The day before the

Derby I saw him step on a roofing nail, and I just happened to be there and notice it. I stopped him before he could press down on the nail. And then it came up rain for the Derby, and the track never did dry out. It was soft, perfect for Pensive's tender feet."

While continuing to train for Calumet, Jones assumed the position of general manager of the racing stable in 1947, and the next year he trained his fourth Derby winner, Citation. Actually, Citation was trained by Jones' son, Jimmy, but the colt went down in the program—and the record book—as Ben's starter for that race, thus tying him with H. J. "Derby Dick" Thompson for most Derby victories by a trainer.

The elder Jones spared no superlatives in describing Citation. "Man o' War? Citation is a better horse," Jones said. "Two things make Citation a great horse. First, he is far above average intelligence. Secondly, he can run any kind of race—come from behind or make his own pace. I've tried to fault him, but I just can't find any holes. He's the best."

Jones appeared back on the Derby scene in 1949 and started Ponder, who went off at 16–1 odds. Before the race, Jones said, "That poor little old horse of mine, he ain't got no more chance'n a Shetland pony. I'd be so happy if I could get just a little piece of the purse." Ponder, a son of Pensive, got the biggest piece of the purse, rallying from last place to win by three lengths and provide Jones with his fifth Derby success.

Jones worked his Derby magic for the last time three years later with Hill Gail, a temperamental son of Bull Lea. Hill Gail was timed in 2:01³/₅, which at that time tied him with Middleground (1950) for the second-fastest Derby in history.

Most trainers would give anything to win a Derby—and Jones won six of them from just eleven starters. He also trained two runners-up, Pot o' Luck in 1945 and Coaltown in 1948, and one third-place finisher, Faultless in 1947. His other two starters, Technician in 1939 and Fanfare in 1951, both ran fifth.

He truly was a master at winning the Derby.

Jimmy Jones trained two Derby winners himself, Iron Liege (1957) and Tim Tam (1958). They formed quite a team, Plain Ben and Jimmy, and it was said that together they made the "Jones Boys" as famous as another pair of Missouri boys, the "James boys," were infamous.

Plain Ben compiled a brilliant record at Kentucky tracks. He held the undisputed lead in the trainer standings at five Keeneland meetings (springs of 1940, 1941, 1947 and 1948, and fall of 1940), and he tied for the top spot once (spring, 1953). He was the sole leader among trainers at five Churchill Downs meetings (springs 1937–40, and fall of 1939) and tied for that honor at two other meetings (springs of 1941 and 1947).

He won stakes thirteen times at Keeneland races. Among his Keeneland successes, he triumphed in the Blue Grass Stakes three times (Ocean Wave, 1943; Faultless, 1947; and Coaltown, 1948), in the Ashland twice (Bewitch, 1948, and Real Delight, 1952, second division), and in the Breeders' Futurity once (Whirlaway, 1940).

At Churchill Downs, he rang up victories in twenty-one stakes. Besides his six Derby triumphs, Jones sent out four Kentucky Oaks winners—Nellie L. (1943), Wistful (1949), Real Delight (1952), and Bubbley (1953).

Jones retired in 1960 and died the following year at the age of seventy-eight. "Ben Jones always will be closely intertwined with the Kentucky Derby," Churchill Downs president Wathen Knebelkamp said at the time of the horseman's death. "He's one of the people who made the Derby."

9

A Touch of Derby in the Orient

DANCER'S IMAGE HAS ALWAYS caught the attention of the wives—first Peter Fuller's and then Koichiro Hayata's.

If it hadn't been for his wife, Bostonian Fuller would never have been at the 1968 Kentucky Derby with Dancer's Image, a colt who was well known for his stretch runs and bad ankles. As soon as Fuller's trainer, Lou Cavalaris, saw those ankles when Dancer's Image was a youngster, he said the horse would never be able to hold up under training.

"I don't like those ankles," Cavalaris told Fuller.

Fuller thus decided to sell Dancer's Image, putting the colt in a Florida Breeders' Sales Company auction at Hialeah. The bidding on the son of Native Dancer soon reached twenty-five thousand dollars, and Fuller's wife, Joan, who had always liked Dancer's Image and never wanted him sold in the first place, couldn't keep her eyes off him as he stepped around the ring.

"My, look how alert he is," Joan said. "He's so strong-looking, and he's got a beautiful color. Gee, he's a neat horse." Then she nudged her husband. Getting the message, Fuller bid twenty-six thousand dollars, and just like that he was still the owner of Dancer's Image.

Years later, Hayata's wife, Yukiko (or Yuki), persuaded her husband, a prominent Japanese horseman, to buy Dancer's Image. Except she wasn't close enough to him to nudge him. They were thousands of miles from each other.

First let Hayata explain: "I like the Native Dancer line very much, so I bought Dancer. At that time, I bought Satingo, by Petingo. I saw Dancer in France after I bought Satingo. I liked both stallions. I couldn't decide whether to buy two; then I called overseas to Japan to my wife to discuss. She said she loved Dancer more than Satingo. So I bought Dancer."

Mrs. Hayata elaborated: "He was interested in buying Satingo, but I wanted to buy Dancer's Image, and I told him to buy Dancer's Image." With a laugh, she added, "We got into a real fight, but we bought two (Satingo and Dancer's Image). We're very happy to have Dancer's Image and own him. I love him very much."

During his days in the Orient, Dancer's Image has stood at Hayata's farm, which is tucked away in a remote area of Japan, close to the Pacific Ocean on the island of Hokkaido, which is north of Honshu, the main island of Japan. Hokkaido is the thoroughbred breeding center of Japan. Certain parts of the area, with black fences running alongside the farmland, resemble the Bluegrass country of Kentucky.

Hayata and his wife both are veterinarians, and both speak English. Each graduated from the Kitasato University Veterinary School, Koichiro then going to the Canada Nashville Stud, Ontario, to study for two years, and Yukiko attending the University of California at Davis for two years.

Dancer's Image, bred in Maryland, has been a much-traveled stallion. Following his retirement in 1968, he stood at Glade Valley Farms near Frederick, Maryland, for his first five years at stud (1969–73). Dancer's Image then went to Ireland and took up residence at the Killeen Castle Stud, standing there for three breeding seasons. Next, he was off to France, where he stood in 1977, 1978, and 1979 at the Haras du Quesnay, a stud farm ten kilometers from Deauville.

While he was remembered for his come-from-behind victories in the mile-and-a-fourth Kentucky Derby, the mile-and-an-eighth Wood Memorial, and the mile-and-a-sixteenth Governor's Gold Cup, Dancer's Image sired a number of good sprinters in Europe, including the talented filly Lianga, 1975 champion French sprinter; Saritamer, 1974 top-weighted sprinter in England; and Godswalk, 1977 International Handicap's top-ranked three-year-old sprinter who turned out to be a good sire himself.

After being purchased by Hayata, Dancer's Image arrived in Japan in the fall of 1979. He has proven to be quite popular with Japanese breeders. In 1983, he was Japan's leading first-year stallion. In terms of money won at Japan Racing Association tracks, he ranked as the country's No. 20 sire in both 1985 and 1986, and in 1987 he climbed to fourteenth. In 1988, he ranked twenty-seventh, and in 1989 he was twenty-second.

Just like some guys like blondes and others brunettes, Dancer's Image has a preference. "He loves gray mares especially," Koichiro Hayata noted.

The stallion is doing quite well in his old days. He's virtually all white, quite a contrast from his gray coat during his racing days.

Dancer's Image has always been a favorite of mine. I bet on him in the 1968 Derby, and, to this day, a small jockey statue in my backyard is painted in Fuller's colors—green and gold—in honor of the horse and the man who had the Derby taken away from them.

The last time I saw Dancer's Image in the United States he was standing quietly in Barn 24 at Churchill Downs in the early hours of the Wednesday morning following the 1968 Derby. It had been announced the previous day that the horse had tested positive for the then-illegal phenylbutazone. As a sportswriter for *The Courier-Journal*, I

Dancer's Image romped around his paddock on Hokkaido in 1987.
(Courtesy Jim Bolus)

Koichiro and Yukiko Hayata with Dancer's Image in 1988.

visited the barn with colleague Billy Reed, and we found security to be anything but tight. It seems a seventy-two-year-old guard was snoozing on the job in Barn 24.

At any rate, I can still remember a red light glowing in the colt's stall. So you can imagine my feeling of *déjà vu* when, in 1987, I visited Dancer's Image in Japan and saw that he was close to infrared-ultraviolet lights in his barn. The lights were positioned in the ceiling outside his stall, and he received infrared-ultraviolet therapy each evening for five to ten minutes. "It is good for old stallion," Koichiro Hayata said.

In 1987, Dancer's Image looked and acted younger than his age. He was exercised every morning for thirty minutes with stud farm manager Kenichi Furusawa, a short, stocky fellow, astride him either in the stallion's paddock or along a grassy stretch lined by cherry trees and running next to a two-lane paved highway that bordered the farm. Dancer's Image has had quite a few riders climb aboard him during his lifetime—nine different jockeys in his twenty-four-race career—and in 1987 it was Furusawa riding the old horse. Asked what kind of steed Dancer's Image was to ride, Furusawa replied through an interpreter: "He feels very comfortable."

Dancer's Image hadn't forgotten what it was like to set sail, his mane breezing in the wind. He liked to gallop about, as evidenced by two well-worn paths in his paddock, one running alongside the fenceline and the other—a circular one—in the middle.

On the day that I saw him late that spring, the stallion looked as if he was thoroughly enjoying himself in the Far East. He was active and healthy and in good condition.

Led to his paddock, which was right behind the stud barn, he bounced along, friskily tossing his head in the air. Once in the paddock, he whinnied and took off into a corner, bent over to graze a bit, and then looked majestically over the fence. Furusawa came over and fed Dancer's Image some long blades of grass.

The stallion took off again, going down the fenceline, and then stopped at the other end of the paddock. Furusawa called for him, and Dancer's Image quickly galloped to the manager. "Ho, ho, ho," said Furusawa, who then whistled. Dancer's Image suddenly stopped. Called to the fence, he came over and was fed some more grass by Furusawa.

Unlike so many Japanese stallions, Dancer's Image seemed to know how to pose for pictures—ears up, alert look. Where it took handlers quite a while to get a good many Japanese stallions to stand correctly for photographs, Dancer's Image struck an impressive pose almost instantly.

When Fuller saw pictures taken of Dancer's Image in Japan, he said, "It's amazing how much Dancer looks like his dad at a similar age."

Dancer's Image holds a special place in the heart of Fuller's sister, Lydia F. Bottomley. "You will never know how much I loved that horse and how much I miss him," she said.

On a visit to Japan again in 1990, I made it a point to drop by and see Dancer's Image. He still looked fine to me, although his age seemed to be telling more on him.

When it came to breeding, he still was active. Like Ol' Man River, he just keeps rollin' along.

Teddy Okabe, deputy general manager of the Japan Racing Association's media and publicity department, reported in 1992 the following item appearing in a Japanese sports newspaper:

"Oirakuno Koi Jouju."

(Translation: Love affair between aged[s] has been made.)

Here's the story on that love affair: At the age of twenty-seven, Dancer's Image was the oldest active stallion in Japan in 1992. Among those bred to him that year was Keikou Laina, an Anglo-Arab mare who was twenty-three. She was confirmed to be in foal.

Okabe noted that if the offspring were born safely in the spring of 1993, "it will make a new record for old parents with the total age of *fifty-two!*"

Dancer's Image covered twenty-eight mares in 1992—twenty-four thoroughbreds and four Anglo-Arabs.

"Dancer is doing fine," said Yuki Hayata in 1992. "He loves mint candies very much. So I never forget to buy souvenir mint candies when I visit Kentucky."

If this story started on an ironic note of the two wives playing such a key role in the fate of this horse, then it should end with even more irony: The southern part of Hokkaido, where Dancer's Image lives, is virtually the same latitude as Boston, Massachusetts, where Fuller lives.

Moreover, consider this twist of fate: Dancer's Image was stripped of his Derby victory due to the presence of the then-illegal Butazolidin in his system, and Forward Pass, the second-place finisher who ultimately was recognized as the winner of the race, ended up in Japan, too.

In 1978, Forward Pass arrived in Japan and began stud duty at Nishiyama Farm, about a forty-minute drive from where Dancer's Image began standing for the 1980 season.

Forward Pass died of colic on December 1, 1980, at Nishiyama Farm. He was buried there, and a marker was placed over his grave.

Thus, the first two finishers in the controversial '68 Derby both wound up in Japan, just forty minutes apart. So near to each other in Japan, so far from Churchill Downs, where they finished a length and a half apart in the 1968 Run for the Roses.

Sunday Silence in "The Land of the Rising Sun"

In a 1990 interview in Tokyo, Teruya Yoshida, eldest son of Shadai Farm owner Zenya Yoshida, said: "We would like to make our farm Claiborne Farm in Japan."

Shadai Farm, with its high standards, already *is* the Claiborne Farm of Japan. Shadai has a rich tradition, a fine broodmare band, and a lineup of blue-blooded stallions.

And now it has Sunday Silence.

The elder Yoshida purchased 1989 Kentucky Derby winner and Horse of the Year Sunday Silence in 1990 to join his stallion roster at Shadai.

Sunday Silence wasn't the first Kentucky Derby winner to go to Japan. But he was the best one—by far.

Five other Derby winners preceded Sunday Silence to Japan, but none of them was a Horse of the Year. None of them boasted a great racing record. None of them had the promising future at stud that Sunday Silence had when he arrived in Japan.

Those five were Iron Liege (1957), Chateaugay (1963), Kauai King (1966), Forward Pass (1968), and Dust Commander (1970).

Teruya Yoshida doesn't need anybody from America to tell him the names of these Derby winners. He knows them by heart, saying: "Dust Commander was a little bit successful—but not as much as we expected. He had produced some good ones in America. But before that, Kauai King, Iron Liege, Forward Pass, those horses came to Japan with unsuccessful results as stallions. There was no chance we could make it that way. They came to Japan with just a title—the Kentucky Derby winner.

"So now we understand. Those horses are no good anymore, even in Japan. Before, we thought the horse with those titles like Kentucky Derby or Epsom Derby winner, we could make some business with just that title, even if he's unsuccessful there as a stallion. But nowadays, by computer or with many publications, we know which stallions produce which winners. So now we are more careful about which stallions we should buy. Our standards become very high now. We would like to make our standards of thoroughbred quality one of the best in the world."

Yoshida said that his father purchased Sunday Silence for $11 million. The elder Yoshida paid a reported $2.5 million for a quarter interest in the horse in March of 1990 and then bought out his partners—Arthur B. Hancock III, trainer Charlie Whittingham, and Dr. Ernest Gaillard—in the late summer of that year.

Sunday Silence then was syndicated, thirty shares retained by Yoshida and thirty sold to syndicate members, all Japanese. "We had to say no to many people," Teruya Yoshida said. "Many, many people would like to have shares.

"We sold from the base of $11 million," he added, noting that a reported syndication price of $18 million "included interest and insurance for five years," as well as a transacting fee. "We had to borrow money from the bank, and the bank asked us to insure the horse in case something happened. So we owe that kind of money for five years for this horse.

"All Japanese are very excited, very happy to have Sunday Silence in Japan. Big crowds are at the racetrack in Japan now—it's a *very popular* sport in Japan now—and naturally our breeders have a kind of duty to provide one of the best bloodlines in the world. That is a good reward to the fans who support the racing. And they are very happy because they'll see Sunday Silence's offspring running in Japanese racing."

Shadai Farm is a showplace that reminds American visitors of the finest thoroughbred nurseries in the United States. "I've known the Yoshidas for twenty years,"

Hancock said after Sunday Silence was sold. "They're great people, and they have a great farm. The horse will be happy."

And the Rest . . .

Taking a look at the other Kentucky Derby winners who went to Japan . . .

•Iron Liege arrived in Japan from France in December 1967 and stood in Hokkaido. On December 14, 1971, he died at Shizunai Stallion Station, Japan Light-Breed Horse Association.

•Chateaugay was purchased in January 1972 by brothers Kazuo and Yoshimitsu Fujii. He sired 541 foals in Japan, including eleven stakes winners, and died on May 9, 1985, at Ohtsuka Bokujo in Hokkaido.

•Kauai King, who arrived in Japan from England in January 1974, originally stood at Sagamore Farm in Maryland from 1967 through the 1971 breeding season. He then was sent to Hamilton Stud near Newmarket, England. After two years in England, he went to Japan for the 1974 breeding season. The twenty-six-year-old horse died of old age on January 24, 1989, at Maekawa Stallion Center in Hokkaido, where he had been standing prior to his retirement from stud duty.

•Forward Pass was sold to Nishiyama Farm in Hokkaido in November 1977 and left Calumet Farm on January 4, 1978. He sired eighty-five horses in Japan, including two important two-year-old race winners. He died in Japan at the age of fifteen.

•Dust Commander started his stud career at Golden Chance Farm, Paris, Kentucky, standing there for the 1971–73 breeding seasons before departing for Japan in September 1973, when his first foals were yearlings. He stood at Nitta Bokujo in Chiba Prefecture (neighboring Tokyo) for six seasons, then was returned to the United States, arriving at Gainesway Farm in the fall of 1979. He was moved to Springland Farm, Paris, Kentucky, in November 1986 and was destroyed there October 7, 1991, due to the infirmities of old age.

Note: Dancer's Image died in Japan on December 25, 1992.

Trainer Vic Sovinski led Venetian Way to the winner's circle following the 1960 Kentucky Derby. Thirty years later, trainer Carl Nafzger held Derby winner Unbridled in the Churchill Downs stable area the day after the big race. (Courtesy Keeneland-Meadors, 1960, and Jim Bolus, 1990)

10

History Does Repeat Itself

THE 1990 TRIPLE CROWN RACES, in a lot of ways, were carbon copies of the 1960 Triple Crown classics.

The 1990 Kentucky Derby boasted the Big Two of Mister Frisky (1.90–1) and Summer Squall (2.10–1). The 1960 Derby had the Big Two of Tompion (1.10–1) and Bally Ache (1.70–1). Both favorites had won the Santa Anita Derby (Mister Frisky by four and a half lengths, Tompion by four).

Each Derby winner—Unbridled in 1990 and Venetian Way in 1960—started off his three-year-old season in Florida and then raced once in Kentucky before the Derby. Going into the Derby, each colt won one race and finished in the money in two others as a three-year-old.

Each Derby winner lost his previous start to the horse who would finish second in the Churchill Downs classic. Unbridled was third in the Blue Grass, three and three-quarter lengths behind the victorious Summer Squall, and Venetian Way was second in the Stepping Stone Purse, three and one-quarter lengths in back of Bally Ache. The '90 Blue Grass and the '60 Stepping Stone had the same numbers of starters: five.

Both Derbies had a scratch—Country Day in 1990, Hillsborough in 1960.

Unbridled captured the '90 Derby by three and a half lengths, the same winning margin for Venetian Way in '60.

149

The second choice finished second both years, Summer Squall in '90 and Bally Ache in '60. There was a big gap between second and third both years—six lengths separating Summer Squall and Pleasant Tap in 1990 and seven and a half lengths between Bally Ache and Victoria Park in 1960.

The similarities continued.

Both Derby winners wore the No. 7 saddlecloth, both had prominent blazes, and both carried blue silks (light blue and yellow for Unbridled, blue and white for Venetian Way).

There's more. The owners of the two winners—Isaac Blumberg (Venetian Way) and Frances Genter (Unbridled)—had the same number of letters in their names—thirteen. Ditto for the trainers—Vic Sovinski (Venetian Way) and Carl Nafzger (Unbridled)—eleven. And the jockeys, too—Bill Hartack (Venetian Way) and Craig Perret (Unbridled)—eleven.

Moreover, the temperature patterns for the two days were similar, with a high (sixty-three degrees in 1990 and sixty-four degrees in 1960) at midnight of Derby morning. Both Derby Days also had rain, and both races were run on "good" tracks. Venetian Way's time of 2:02²/₅ was the best ever for an off track in the Derby until Unbridled bettered it with his 2:02.

History continued to repeat itself in the Preakness when the Kentucky Derby runner-up came back to win the Pimlico classic as the second choice, Summer Squall triumphant by two and a quarter lengths and Bally Ache by four lengths.

The 1990 Belmont completed the history-repeating act. Like 1960, the 1990 Belmont had the Derby winner but not the Preakness winner. And, like 1960, when the English-bred Celtic Ash won the Belmont, "The Test of the Champion" in 1990 was won by a foreign-bred, Go and Go, who was foaled in Ireland.

What's more, both Belmont winners led by a half-length at the stretch call and went on to triumph by big margins, Go and Go winning by eight and a fourth and Celtic Ash by five and a half. Both winners were fourth choices in the betting, Go and Go going off at 7.50–1 and Celtic Ash at 8.40–1. The favorite in both races ran fourth, Unbridled at 1.10–1 in 1990 and Tompion at .85–1 in 1960.

In both years of the series, the Kentucky Derby winner later finished second in one leg of the Triple Crown (Unbridled in the Preakness, Venetian Way in the Belmont) but ran out of the money in another leg (Unbridled fourth in the Belmont, Venetian Way fifth in the Preakness).

The combined winning margins for the three races in 1990: fourteen lengths; for 1960: thirteen lengths.

Bally Ache, who ran second in the Derby and won the Preakness, finished ahead of Venetian Way in seven of their nine career meetings. Summer Squall, who ran second in the Derby and won the Preakness, finished ahead of Unbridled in four of their six encounters.

And who says history doesn't repeat itself?

Affirmed (left) and Alydar, rivals on the racetrack, were the closest of neighbors for several years in retirement, occupying adjoining stalls in the stud barn at Calumet Farm. (Courtesy Dick Martin, Louisville, Kentucky)

11

Affirmed and Alydar, Racing's Greatest Rivalry

NOT MUCH SEPARATED Affirmed and Alydar on the race-track. Although Affirmed held a 7–3 advantage in their ten meetings (one of Alydar's triumphs came by way of a disqualification), these two rivals were involved in five races in which a half-length or less was the difference between them. Their ten races totaled ten and five-sixteenths miles, and at the end of all that running (54,450 feet, to be exact), Affirmed finished ahead of Alydar by only about four and a half lengths—or approximately thirty-eight feet. The difference between these two probably would have been less than four and a half lengths had Alydar not met interference in their last meeting, the Travers, a race in which he was forced to drop back three to six lengths after Affirmed cut him off at the end of the backstretch.

These two colts met six times as two-year-olds and then faced each other in four races as three-year-olds. Affirmed won the 1978 Triple Crown (Kentucky Derby, Preakness, and Belmont), and Alydar is the only horse in history to finish second in all three of those classic races.

"You can go back through racing history," the late Louisville newspaperman Mike Barry once said, "and there's never been anything like this that went on for two seasons—as two-year-olds and as three-year-olds. I've never found anything similar to it in all the reading I've done where two horses battled each other for two seasons."

153

DATE	TRACK	RACE (distance)	FINISH	MARGIN between the two
June 15, 1977	Belmont Park	Youthful (5 1/2 furlongs)	Affirmed 1st, Alydar 5th	5 lengths
July 6, 1977	Belmont Park	Great American (5 1/2 furlongs)	Alydar 1st, Affirmed 2nd	3 1/2 lengths
Aug. 27, 1977	Saratoga	Hopeful (6 1/2 furlongs)	Affirmed 1st, Alydar 2nd	half-length
Sept. 10, 1977	Belmont Park	Futurity (7 furlongs)	Affirmed 1st, Alydar 2nd	nose
Oct. 15, 1977	Belmont Park	Champagne (1 mile)	Alydar 1st, Affirmed 2nd	1 1/4 lengths
Oct. 29, 1977	Laurel	Laurel Futurity (1 1/16 miles)	Affirmed 1st, Alydar 2nd	neck
May 6, 1978	Churchill Downs	Kentucky Derby (1 1/4 miles)	Affirmed 1st, Alydar 2nd	1 1/2 lengths
May 20, 1978	Pimlico	Preakness (1 3/16 miles)	Affirmed 1st, Alydar 2nd	neck
June 10, 1978	Belmont Park	Belmont (1 1/2 miles)	Affirmed 1st, Alydar 2nd	head
Aug. 19, 1978	Saratoga	Travers (1 1/4 miles)	*Alydar 1st, Affirmed 2nd	1 3/4 lengths

*Affirmed finished first in the Travers but was disqualified to second, and Alydar was moved up to the top spot.

A footnote to the Affirmed-Alydar rivalry: In retirement, Alydar returned to his birthplace, Calumet Farm at Lexington, Kentucky, and proved to be more successful at stud than Affirmed. He sired such standouts as Alysheba, the 1987 Kentucky Derby winner and 1988 Horse of the Year; Criminal Type, the 1990 Horse of the Year; Easy Goer, the 1988 champion two-year-old colt and 1989 Belmont winner; Turkoman, champion older male of 1986; Althea, champion two-year-old filly of 1983; Miss Oceana, a multiple stakes winner, and Saratoga Six, who was unbeaten in four two-year-old starts before an injury ended his career in 1984.

Affirmed, the Horse of the Year in 1978 and 1979, began his stud career at Spendthrift Farm near Lexington, standing there for seven breeding seasons. Then, in an ironic twist of fate, he was moved in the fall of 1986 from Spendthrift to Calumet Farm to join up once again with Alydar.

Thus, these two old racing rivals became the closest of neighbors, residing right next door to one another in the same spotless stud barn at Calumet Farm. Not only that, but their paddocks were across from each other, with a farm road running in between. That meant that throughout the day Affirmed and Alydar were usually near to one another, which seemed only appropriate considering that they were never all that far apart at the end of their many racing duels.

Alydar was destroyed in the fall of 1990, the year that he ranked as North America's leading sire by progeny earnings. In the summer of 1991, Affirmed was moved to Jonabell Farm.

Crozier a "Bridesmaid" to Carry Back

Crozier was a talented horse, but Carry Back proved to be his nemesis during their fierce rivalry. Like Affirmed and Alydar, these two horses battled each other ten times. Carry Back finished ahead of Crozier in seven of those races. The total difference in the ten races was seventeen and one-quarter lengths in Carry Back's favor. In their seven meetings in 1961, they carried the same weights. But in three 1962 encounters, Carry Back packed forty-six more pounds than Crozier.

In 1961, Crozier suffered three of his losses to Carry Back by a total of a mere length. Carry Back overtook Crozier to win the Flamingo by a head, with a difference of

$58,410 between first- and second-place purse money. Carry Back nailed Crozier for a head victory in the Florida Derby, which provided $55,100 more to the winner than to the runner-up. And in the Kentucky Derby, it was the same story. Carry Back ran down Crozier for a three-quarter-length triumph that meant a difference of $95,500 between winning and running second. Losing those three races by eight or nine feet cost Crozier $209,010 in purse money, not to mention a world of prestige.

Jack Price, who trained Carry Back for his wife, Katherine, recalled years later that Fred Hooper, the owner of Crozier, held a grudge for a long time. "Fred Hooper's really mellowed," Price said. "He's forgotten, I guess, that he used to get mad."

With a grin, Price went on: "Maybe I'd be the same way if Crozier was beating us heads, necks, noses for all the three-year-old stakes. He didn't talk to me for years. He was really mad. But that's all forgotten now."

Sunday Silence and Easy Goer . . .
Neighbors and Rivals

They were born four days apart at neighboring thoroughbred farms just outside Paris, Kentucky. They grew up close together, within a mile or so of each other during one period of their lives, and then on the racetrack, they were close again, hooking up in some memorable battles in 1989.

Sunday Silence and Easy Goer. Easy Goer and Sunday Silence.

These two colts, the best runners in America in 1989, will forever be linked together. You won't be able to think about one without the other entering your mind. Just like Affirmed and Alydar.

Sunday Silence was born March 25, 1986, at Stone Farm. Four days earlier, Easy Goer had been foaled at

Claiborne Farm. From early October of 1986 through the first four months of 1987, they were virtual neighbors, living within about a mile of each other on the west side of Paris, Kentucky. Sunday Silence romped around those days in a pasture at the Walnut Lee section of Stone Farm, staying there until the first of May 1987. Easy Goer was raised in the front field of Claiborne Farm's Raceland No. 2 section, remaining there until August 1987.

In their first battle, the Kentucky Derby, Sunday Silence won by two and a half lengths over second-place Easy Goer on a muddy track. Two weeks later in the Preakness, Sunday Silence nosed out Easy Goer in a torrid stretch battle. The Preakness was acclaimed the "Race of the Year."

Then, in the mile-and-a-half Belmont Stakes, it was Easy Goer's turn, and he came rolling home on top by eight lengths.

Their final meeting was the Breeders' Cup Classic, and Sunday Silence won this one by a long neck over the closing Easy Goer.

So that was it . . . three wins for Sunday Silence, one for Easy Goer.

At the conclusion of the Affirmed-Alydar rivalry, it was hard to dispute which one was the better runner. Affirmed held a 7–3 advantage in their meetings and was the superior runner. Not by much maybe, but he still had Alydar's number. The same with the Carry Back-Crozier rivalry. Carry Back was the better racehorse, no question about it.

The Sunday Silence-Easy Goer rivalry, however, wasn't quite as conclusive. Sunday Silence led 3–1 in the rivalry, and his backers didn't think he had anything else to prove. He had outrun Easy Goer in all but one of their meetings. Yet, certain Easy Goer partisans remained loyal to this New York-based runner, convinced that he was the better colt.

Such was the Sunday Silence-Easy Goer rivalry.

Warner L. Jones Jr. accepted the 1990 Eclipse Award of Merit in San Francisco. (Courtesy Stidham & Associates)

Warner L. Jones Jr. (Courtesy Keeneland Association by Bill Straus)

12

Warner L. Jones, Jr.: More Than Fifty Years of Dedication to the Downs

WARNER L. JONES JR. is a man who has left his mark on the thoroughbred industry in more ways than one.

A pillar of the Kentucky thoroughbred establishment, Jones has made a great contribution to the sport by breeding fine horses for more than a half-century, by serving as a Churchill Downs director since 1941, and by remaining active in racing matters throughout the years.

Jones, board chairman at Churchill Downs from 1984–92, established quite a reputation as a breeder of outstanding thoroughbreds. He will long be remembered as the first person to breed a Kentucky Derby winner (Dark Star, 1953), a Kentucky Oaks winner (Nancy Jr., 1967, and Seaside Attraction, 1990, the latter in partnership with Albert G. Clay and Robert N. Clay), and a winner of a Breeders' Cup championship race (Is It True, 1988 Juvenile).

Moreover, Jones and two others bred Seattle Dancer, who sold for a world-record $13.1 million at Keeneland's 1985 July Selected Yearling Sale.

Jones has been influential on many fronts.

He was elected to The Jockey Club in 1971 and in 1992 completed a term on that prestigious body's board of stewards.

In addition, he helped found the American Horse Council, which began in 1969, and was chairman of the board of trustees for that organization in 1978 and 1981.

159

He also has been on Keeneland's board of directors since 1959.

For his distinguished service to thoroughbred racing, Jones received the 1990 Eclipse Award of Merit, the sport's highest accolade.

"He's done everything," said Seth Hancock, president of Claiborne Farm. "He's been so much of a factor on the field, so to speak, with all that he's done as far as actual racing horses and selling horses, but he's done so much off the field with the work that he's done with the American Horse Council and so many of those type of groups that have helped this game stay afloat."

For many years one of the leading breeders in America, Jones is no longer as actively involved in that phase of the industry, having sold most of his breeding stock at a 1987 dispersal. He still owns seven-hundred-acre Hermitage Farm, located near Goshen, Kentucky, where approximately 150 horses reside, about half of them boarders.

Since his dispersal, Jones' emphasis has gone toward racing a stable of horses, and he is having plenty of success at the track. "I'm doing pretty well racing them, and I enjoy it," the native Louisvillian said. "I don't have the pressure of the sale and stuff like that. It's a lot more fun than waiting on a broodmare for eleven months to have a foal and then waiting another year to sell it at the yearling sale and hope the dogs don't chase it through a fence."

Fit for a Queen distinguished herself in Hermitage's colors. Jones purchased the daughter of Fit to Fight in April 1990, and she proceeded to win seven stakes for him, including the Louisville Budweiser Breeders' Cup and the Churchill Downs Budweiser Breeders' Cup, both in 1991.

Jones is strongly identified with Churchill Downs, the track where he has served as director for more than fifty years. Col. M. Lewis Clark, founder of the Kentucky Derby, was a great-great-great uncle of Jones, who began serving as a director at Churchill Downs at a time when Col. Matt Winn was track president. Colonel Winn died in 1949, having seen all of the first seventy-five runnings of the Derby.

"He was a good friend of mine," Jones said. "He was old, and I was young, and I *loved* him. He was the greatest promoter there ever was and the nicest guy. He knew the value of having the press on our side, and he knew that the public wanted to see the movie actors and actresses and celebrities, and he'd make them welcome here."

If Colonel Winn could come back today and Jones could take him on a tour of Churchill Downs, what would be his reaction? "He'd love it," Jones said. "I'd show him the new paddock and the turf course."

To be sure, while still retaining its old charm, Churchill Downs underwent important changes after Jones took over as board chairman in 1984. The Downs, under the aggressive leadership of president Tom Meeker, completed a five-year, $25 million capital-improvement program (1984–89) that included a $2.6 million paddock/tote board complex (first used in the fall of 1986) and $3.2 million for a turf course (opened in the spring of 1987), a new infield tunnel, and refurbishing of the infield presentation stand.

"We got to keep up with the times," Jones said during that period. "Nothing had been spent on this place when we took over in 1984. For a long time, I thought we were sitting on a gold mine but we weren't mining the gold. That was the reason people were coming after us trying to take us over."

Jones has made a lasting mark as a breeder. He sold his first yearling at Saratoga in 1937 and has bred four champions (each in partnership) and two world-record yearlings (one in partnership). The champions bred by Jones: Bold Fascinator (1970 French two-year-old filly, tie),

Northern Trick (1984 European and French three-year-old filly, eleven furlongs and up), Rousillon (1985 French miler), and Woodman (1985 Irish two-year-old colt).

In 1985, Jones sold eight yearlings at the Keeneland July Selected Yearling Sale for $19,470,000, the largest sum received by a single consignor in the history of that auction.

And, of course, he'll always be known as the man who bred the winners of the Derby, the Oaks, and a Breeders' Cup championship race.

All four paid handsomely, Dark Star returning $51.80 on a two-dollar-win bet, Nancy Jr. $61.80, Is It True $20.40, and Seaside Attraction $18.20 (as part of a three-horse entry).

All four beat odds-on favorites who were champions. Native Dancer, coupled with Social Outcast and favored at 7–10, finished second in the 1953 Derby. Native Dancer was Horse of the Year in one poll at two, champion three-year-old of 1953, and Horse of the Year again at four. Furl Sail, also a 7–10 favorite, ran third in the 1967 Oaks and was voted that season's three-year-old filly champion in one poll. Easy Goer, a 3–10 choice, came in second in the 1988 Breeders' Cup Juvenile and won the Eclipse Award as champion two-year-old colt. Go for Wand, the 1–5 favorite who was champion two-year-old filly of 1989 and champion three-year-old filly of 1990, finished second in the 1990 Oaks.

Looking back on his many accomplishments, Jones said that he received "more kick" from breeding 1953 Derby winner Dark Star than he did from selling the $13.1 million yearling. "Money isn't everything," Jones said.

Speaking of money, Jones doesn't believe the $13.1 million record will ever be broken. "There's no horse on earth worth that much," he said. "I was just lucky as hell two syndicates wanted the same horse and got to bidding against one another. It was at auction, and at auction it takes two bidders to make anything happen. I was just lucky as hell that Wayne Lukas had a syndicate and so did (Robert) Sangster and Vincent O'Brien."

Sangster & Co. acquired the yearling, who was bred by Jones (the consignor), William S. Farish, and William S. Kilroy.

The $13.1 million price was considerably higher than the sixty-five hundred dollars that was paid for Dark Star at Keeneland's 1951 summer sale. Jones sold ten yearlings at that vendue, including eight sired by Royal Gem II (six colts and two fillies).

Three of those Royal Gem II yearling colts "looked as much alike as three peas in a pod," Jones recalled. "Moody Jolley was training for (Harry) Guggenheim. They bought the first one—by Royal Gem out of Isolde, by Bull Dog. And then Moody Jolley came to me during the sale before another one came along and said, 'We bought the wrong horse, and if you'll take him back we'll bid that much more on the next one.' Well, I was nervous and everything, and I said, 'The hell with that. You got long pants on. You bought him, you keep him.' And that turned out to be Dark Star.

"See," Jones went on, "I think that this business is about 90 percent luck. If it wasn't luck, where were all the experts when they sold Seattle Slew (for $17,500)? Where were all the pros that walk around and are so smart? Where was I? Where was anybody?"

Jones also wondered where everybody was when Spectacular Bid sold for thirty-seven thousand dollars or when Genuine Risk went for thirty-two thousand.

"And if it isn't luck," he said, "why didn't that $13 million colt turn into a champion?"

Luck indeed is a big part of the game . . . but Warner L. Jones Jr. has relied not so much on luck but on his knowledge and hard work, plus his love for the sport, to reach his lofty position in the racing world.

13

The Derby's Dirty Dozen

THOROUGHBRED RACING ANNUALLY honors its best horses,
its champions, with Eclipse Awards, the sport's answer to
the Oscars.

But why this obsession with the *best*?

Why shouldn't the worst horses, the chumps, be singled
out, too? Not only singled out, but honored with awards
themselves.

Egads Awards, that is.

The Kentucky Derby has attracted the likes of Secre-
tariat, Citation, Exterminator, Seattle Slew, Count Fleet,
Affirmed, Hindoo, Spectacular Bid, Old Rosebud, War
Admiral, Swaps, and Gallant Fox.

But the Derby also has drawn some awfully slow, awfully
bad, awfully awful horses as well—horses who had no business running in the race but did so usually because of
audacious owners.

This self-proclaimed expert in picking bad horses has
done research and come up with his Derby's Dirty Dozen,
the worst starters ever to compete in this classic race.

The twelve are, in order (drum roll, anybody?): Senecas
Coin, Frank Bird, Orlandwick, Great Redeemer, Kenilworth Lad, Pravus, Dick O'Hara, Saigon Warrior, Fourulla, Layson, Broadway Limited, and Rae Jet.

Let's take a look at these twelve horses (in order of in-
ability) who belong to this fraternity of failures:

Senecas Coin (pulled up in 1949)

This creature was ridden by Jimmy Duff, who encountered a newsman in the paddock after the Derby and asked a reasonable question: "Who win?" Duff certainly had no way of knowing. Senecas Coin, after all, had been pulled up in the neighborhood of a quarter of a mile behind the victorious Ponder. Senecas Coin's Derby race was no fluke, either. He started fifty-three times in his career. He lost fifty-two.

His lone victory came in a 1951 claiming race at River Downs. His winning margin was impressive—five lengths—and his time of 1:48 was a second faster than the track record. The track record for a mile and an eighth, that is. The race Senecas Coin won was only a mile and a sixteenth, though, and his horse-and-buggy time was five and two-fifths seconds slower than the track record.

Senecas Coin continued to race for the next three years. Unlike fine wine, he didn't improve with age. He went 0 for 10 in 1952, 0 for 4 in 1953, and 0 for 2 in 1954.

In his next-to-last race, he ran for a fifteen-hundred-dollar claiming price and finished last in a field of ten. For his grand finale, he ran for a two-thousand-dollar tag and was sent off at 50–1 odds, longest price on the board. But Senecas Coin didn't finish last this time. He came in sixth, thirteen and a quarter lengths behind the winner.

Wonder if that was close enough for his jockey to know who won the race?

Frank Bird (last in 1908)

The foal crop of 1905 brought the racing world such notable horses as Colin, who was never beaten, and Fair Play, a standout runner and the sire of Man o' War. Frank Bird also was a member of that crop. A dishonorable member.

The 1908 Derby did not pull together a classic lineup of thoroughbreds. Somebody had to win the race, and it was Stone Street, who was timed in 2:15⅕ on a heavy track, the Derby's slowest mile and a quarter in history.

Nobody could agree on how far Frank Bird lost the Derby. *The Courier-Journal* said the horse was beaten "about a quarter of a mile," which was an exaggeration. One chart placed Frank Bird forty-five lengths behind the winner at the finish, another put the difference at twenty-nine and a half lengths. One thing was certain: He wasn't close, which was the story of his life.

Frank Bird finished far back in his six career starts, three of which resulted in last-place efforts. Those six races drew a total of fifty-nine starters, all but six of whom finished ahead of Frank Bird.

Orlandwick (last in 1907)

He did manage to win twice in thirty starts, but he showed his true class by being one of those who finished behind Frank Bird.

Great Redeemer (last in 1979)

Great Redeemer was a surprise—or rather a shocking—Derby entrant. Jim James, the colt's trainer, wanted no part of running Great Redeemer in the Derby. He stepped aside (he reportedly resigned before the Derby), only to come back and train Great Redeemer in his next race.

Listed as the trainer of Great Redeemer for the Derby was his owner, one Dr. James A. Mohamed. The horse was a maiden, beaten a total of eighty-four and a half lengths in six starts. He opened at 500–1 in the Derby future book and closed at 1,000–1.

"I'm sure my horse will be running well," Mohamed declared two days before the Derby. "I decided my horse should be there a few days ago. I know because I read the Bible. I pray. I am a born-again Christian."

Asked what had happened between him and James, Mohamed replied: "He decided not to saddle the horse for the Derby, and I don't blame him. He doesn't have that kind of faith. I think differently."

In a column headlined "Mohamed brings a molehill to the Derby," sports editor Billy Reed led off his remarks in *The Courier-Journal* with this thought: "A 'born-again Christian' named Mohamed created an unholy uproar at Churchill Downs by entering a horse with horrible credentials—make that no credentials—in the 105th Kentucky Derby."

Reed went on to refer to Great Redeemer as "a dog" and concluded: "He ought to be entered in the Westminster Show at Madison Square Garden instead of the Kentucky Derby. . . ."

Unlike Reed, sports columnist Mike Barry of *The Louisville Times* refused to denigrate Great Redeemer by calling him a dog.

A turtle is what Barry chose to label Mohammed's horse. "He has a chance to break a Derby record—no horse has ever gone off higher than 294–1," wrote Barry. "If this turtle's odds aren't higher, it will prove Barnum's theory wrong—there's more than one sucker born every minute."

There were enough suckers at the Downs to send Great Redeemer off at odds of only 78–1.

Grover "Bud" Delp, the trainer of Spectacular Bid, said: "I'm afraid I'm going to lap him. My jock's going to have the lead in the stretch, and then he's going to look up and say, 'Uh-oh, there's another one.' He'll probably strip a gear trying to pass him."

Spectacular Bid, of course, didn't lap Great Redeemer. But when Spectacular Bid crossed the finish line, Great Redeemer still had more than a sixteenth of a mile to go. He finished forty-seven and one-quarter lengths behind

Spectacular bid and twenty-five lengths in back of the next-to-last horse, Lot 'o Gold.

After Lot 'o Gold came under the wire, photographers on the track thought the race was over and began to move for the winner's circle. Then along came Great Redeemer. "He was so far back that he almost became the first Derby horse to run over a couple of photographers scrambling to make the winner's circle," Reed wrote. "Of course, he was going so slowly, he probably wouldn't have hurt them."

As it was, one of the photographers actually made it all the way across the track before Great Redeemer finished the race.

"They didn't realize I was that far back, and they ran out in front of me," Great Redeemer's jockey, Richard de Pass, said of the two photographers closest to him. "They were coming—walking or running—and I said, 'Hey!' And they ducked me like. And they laughed when they seen me."

They had reason to laugh. Great Redeemer was strictly a joke.

Not everything connected with this horse's career was a laughing matter, though. Great Redeemer later was sold to Mrs. Patricia Adamo, who along with her husband, Mario, acquired him from Mohamed in a two-horse package deal. "I'm embarrassed to tell you how little it was," she said of the purchase price. "Dr. Mohamed asked me not to reveal it. But, believe me, it was very little.

"The horse, I had been told by the previous owner, had been stabbed by a disgruntled person—by some wacko (sometime after the Derby)," she said. "No one ever knew who did it. He was just found in his stall bleeding the day after the stabbing."

Mrs. Adamo said Mohammed was "very upset" about the stabbing incident. "He was trying to say that this was done because it was him—you know, it was his horse. And this is the story that he gave me; this is why he wanted to sell the horse."

Mrs. Adamo said Great Redeemer suffered a fractured splint bone and that veterinarians believe the injury occurred in the Derby. "The horse isn't all that bad," she said in a 1980 interview. "I don't think he's anywhere near the level of a Spectacular Bid, but he certainly wasn't as bad as everybody was trying to make him look to be. The horse does have some speed. No one will ever know how good he might have been."

In fifty-eight career starts, Great Redeemer did manage to win five races, second among the Dirty Dozen only to Rae Jet's six triumphs.

Hmmm. Wonder if we should have ranked Great Redeemer as the fifth worst Derby starter instead of the fourth?

Kenilworth Lad (last in 1945)

This horse's mother was Tucky Rose.

His trainer was C. P. Rose.

But the Derby didn't come up roses for Kenilworth Lad, who finished fifty-two lengths behind Hoop Jr., the winner.

Kenilworth Lad was accustomed to finishing way back.

He started seventeen times in his career and failed to earn a single dime. He never finished better than sixth. He went 0 for 11 in 1944 and 0 for 5 in 1945. It was almost four full years before Kenilworth Lad raced again. His comeback was short-lived. He broke down during the running of the race.

Racing just never was a rose garden for this horse.

Pravus (last in 1923)

Owner Fred Wieland reportedly ran Pravus in the Derby in order to collect on bets that he had made some months earlier at 4–1 odds that this horse would start in the classic.

Pravus, of course, didn't have a prayer in the Derby.
Pravus died in 1923, leaving behind him career records
that fell short of landing him a place in racing's Hall of
Fame: twenty starts and never a winner. With such a record, this son of The Finn would have been more fittingly
named had he been called The Fink.

Dick O'Hara (last in 1930)

He needed just one thing to win this Derby: A head
start. A big, big head start.

As it was, he had to start with the rest of the field, and
the result was a dismal last-place finish. Dick O'Hara was
no stranger to finishing last. In fifteen career starts, he
finished last seven times. He did manage one victory, but
that was hardly enough to balance out fourteen losses by a
total of $174\frac{3}{4}$ or $185\frac{1}{4}$ lengths.

Dick O'Hara was so badly outclassed in the Derby that
his owner, Chicagoan Pat Joyce, bet on another starter.

But hoping that Dick O'Hara wouldn't finish last, Joyce
promised jockey Newton Barrett five hundred dollars if
he beat just one horse. Though Barrett rode for all he was
worth, Dick O'Hara couldn't get close to the next-to-last
finisher.

According to one story, Joyce put Dick O'Hara in the
Derby for strictly one reason—to win a lottery bet for
some people. Chicago con men, it seems, printed up Derby
lottery tickets with the names of three horses on each
ticket. For a ticket holder to win, all three horses had to
run in the Derby. The catch was that the name of Dick
O'Hara, who had absolutely no business running in the
Derby, appeared on every ticket.

Realizing that they had been taken, the purchasers of
the tickets told Joyce of their plight, and he ran his horse
in the Derby to help them win their prize money. Trouble

was, the con men who organized the ticket scheme blew town. However, so this story went, one of them was caught and prosecuted. He lost the case—but had no money. As a result, nobody collected a penny on the lottery.

Another story suggested that it was gangster George "Bugsy" Moran who was behind the scheme, a coup in which several men working for the circulation department of a Chicago newspaper arranged to sell fifty thousand lottery tickets, each listing Dick O'Hara's name.

All kinds of jokes were made about Dick O'Hara's performance in the Derby. Westbrook Pegler reported to readers of *The Chicago Tribune* that the reason Dick O'Hara didn't appear in the finish picture of the race was "because the Derby was supposed to be a daylight spectacle. The photographers did not take any flash bombs with them, and as the management had not planned for an owl race, the prints of Dick O'Hara's finish came out all black."

Saigon Warrior (last in 1971)

All Saigon Warrior did was lose by seventy-two and a quarter lengths, the farthest any Derby finisher has ever been beaten since the advent of racing charts. Even so, it's not true that they needed lanterns to find Saigon Warrior when he finally dragged himself home. Veteran Louisville newspaperman Mike Barry said they were using flashlights.

In all fairness to Saigon Warrior, it should be noted that he was at a definite disadvantage in the Derby. His jockey, Bobby Parrott, couldn't make the weight, and Saigon Warrior had to carry 127 pounds, one more than each of his opponents. Tremendous burden, that one extra pound.

Saigon Warrior reared in the starting gate and, according to owner-trainer Charles M. Day, suffered an injury and should have been scratched. Actually, if Saigon Warrior had been in his proper place on Derby Day, he never would have had the starting gate mishap. His proper place was in his stall, munching hay, while the deserving horses ran in the Derby.

At any rate, Day said that Saigon Warrior's injury later was diagnosed as a fractured spine. Day said the horse began to experience problems as a result of the injury— "and would fall over and shake. The vets put him to sleep."

A check of Saigon Warrior's career record shows that before the Derby, he was a bad horse. Afterward, whether it was due to the injury that Day said the horse suffered or whatever, Saigon Warrior was no longer just bad.

He was bad, bad, bad.

Fourulla (next to last in 1971)

Some horses just seem to come along in the wrong year. Take Sham. He ran the second-fastest Derby of all time in 1973, yet finished second to Secretariat.

And then there was Fourulla, who was denied a last-place finish by Saigon Warrior.

According to one story appearing on Derby Day in '71, Fourulla "had colic but a few days back." However, owner-trainer Art Sullivan pronounced Fourulla as "'positively recovered' and sees no reason why the colt cannot get the 1¼ miles," the story noted.

Sullivan was right about Fourulla's ability to run a mile and a quarter. The colt could do it. It was just a question of how long it took him.

The silks Fourulla carried to the post were listed as green—a green "S" on gold ball, gold sleeves, and green cap. Rather than an "S," an "SOS" would have been more appropriate. This overmatched colt needed all the help he could get.

He finished fifty-eight and one-quarter lengths back (flashlights for him, too), which would have been good (or

Broadway Limited, with Frank Coltiletti up, sold for $65,000 as a yearling in 1928 and never won in nine starts. "He was nuthin'," said Coltiletti, who rode this son of Man o' War in three races. "He wasn't worth four dollars. They give $65,000 for that bum. He wasn't worth a quarter. He was no count. At least Broadway Limited ran consistent races with Coltiletti aboard. In the three races that Coltiletti rode him, Broadway Limited finished sixth, sixth, and sixth."
(Courtesy Keeneland-Cook)

bad) enough for last place had it not been for Saigon Warrior.

Fourulla never raced again after the Derby, meaning that he retired with an 0-for-5 record, meaning that he lost his five races by a total of eighty-three lengths, and meaning that he had a very meaningless career.

Layson (third in 1905)

How could a third-place finisher be so bad? Easy. There were only three starters.

One race does not a career make, and Layson shouldn't be judged on the Derby alone. Actually, his career record produced both good news and bad news. The good news: He won three times. The bad: He lost eighty-eight.

Broadway Limited (also ran in 1930)

Sold for sixty-five thousand dollars as a yearling, never won in nine starts, never finished in the money, never earned a penny. Never should have run in the Derby.

Rae Jet (last in 1969)

On the afternoon of May 3, 1969, Rae Jet paraded onto the Churchill Downs track before a national television audience. This great-grandson of Man o' War was ready to take on Majestic Prince, Arts and Letters, Dike, Top Knight, and three others in the $155,700 Kentucky Derby. Among the spectators in the crowd of 106,333 were none other than President Richard Nixon and two men—Gerald Ford and Ronald Reagan—who later would take up residence in the White House.

Almost four years later, Rae Jet was competing in another race that had several things in common with the Derby. It was held at a distance of about a mile and a quarter, it was in the spring, and it was in Louisville.

Only this race was on the Oxmoor Steeplechase program, not at Churchill Downs. And there were no horses the caliber of Majestic Prince or Arts and Letters in the race. And there was no President Nixon, nor any future presidents, in the small Sunday gathering of three thousand. And the purse was peanuts—two hundred dollars. No national television either.

Surely, this race (which was on the flat, not over jumps) would be a piece of cake for a horse who once ran in the Kentucky Derby.

Surely, Rae Jet wouldn't embarrass his stable by finishing behind any of his little-known opponents in this nothing race.

Surely, Rae Jet would not—*could not*—lose this race.

Surely, you jest.

Meet Rae Jet, the crab.

Breaking from an open area rather than the conventional starting gate, Rae Jet unseated his rider at the start. It was a lost weekend all the way around for Rae Jet, who had finished fifth a day earlier at Beulah Park.

"He never has started loose like this," his owner, R. E. Harris, said after the Oxmoor debacle. "A horse came over on him at the start, and he shied away from the horse."

Excuses, excuses.

It didn't matter whether he started from a gate or in an open field, Rae Jet was strictly a bad actor. He was such an ill-behaved horse that during his inglorious career he bolted three times, wheeled twice, and lost his rider twice.

Rae Jet was up to no such tricks in the Derby, though. The only trick was on those who bet on the gray gelding. A total of $38,814 was foolishly wagered on Rae Jet in the Derby's win, place, and show pools. Sent off at 70–1 odds, Rae Jet finished forty-two and a half lengths behind the winner, Majestic Prince.

Jockey Bobby Howard tried to offer an alibi for Rae Jet's performance in the Derby. "The big crowd got him all stirred up, and he was rank," Howard said. "When they let out that roar, 'They're off,' it got to him. I wouldn't mind riding him again . . . but in different company."

Come on, Bobby. The crowd was no excuse. Didn't the other seven horses hear the same noise? It didn't matter whether Rae Jet was running in front of 106,333 fans or 6,333, he was still a nut.

DERBY'S DIRTY DOZEN

	HORSE (DERBY YEAR)	FINISH	LOSING MARGIN	CAREER RECORD STARTS	1	2	3
1.	Senecas Coin (1949)	Pulled up	—	53	1	5	3
2.	Frank Bird (1908)	Last	29 1/2 or 45	6	0	0	0
3.	Orlandwick (1907)	Last	16 1/2 or 17 1/2 lengths	30	2	2	4
4.	Great Redeemer (1979)	Last	47 1/4 lengths	58	5	2	8
5.	Kenilworth Lad (1945)	Last	52 lengths	17	0	0	0
6.	Pravus (1923)	Last	28 1/2 or 43 lengths	20	0	3	4
7.	Dick O'Hara (1930)	Last	24 3/4 or 35 1/4 lengths	15	1	3	0
8.	Saigon Warrior (1971)	Last	72 1/4 lengths	34	2	4	4
9.	Fourulla (1971)	Next-to-last	58 1/4 lengths	5	0	1	1
10.	Layson (1905)	Last	13 or 23 lengths	91	3	8	12
11.	Broadway Limited (1930)	9th or next-to-last	13 1/2 or 15 1/4 lengths	9	0	0	0
12.	Rae Jet (1969)	Last	42 1/2 lengths	85	6	12	11

14

Black Jockeys:
Isaac Murphy & Co.

A SPORTS FAN CAN ATTEND a professional basketball game
these days and he'll see black athletes excel in the three
Ds—dribbling, dunking, and dominating. He can go to a
football game where blacks are zigging and zagging their
way for touchdowns or to a baseball game where blacks
steal second base quicker than you can say Jackie Robinson. Or he can attend a boxing match where two blacks are
in the ring, one trying to slug it out while the other floats
like a butterfly and stings like a bee.

Yet if a sports fan goes to the thoroughbred horse races,
he'll notice black grooms—and even perhaps black trainers
and owners—but he'll likely go all day without seeing the
first black jockey. A good bet would be that he'd see a
woman jockey first.

It hasn't always been that way.

In the late 1800s and early in this century, black jockeys rode often, and they rode to win. The early history
of the Kentucky Derby reflects the extent to which black
jockeys were dominant. Fourteen of the fifteen jockeys
in the inaugural Derby of 1875 were black, and fifteen
of the first twenty-eight Derbies were won by black riders.
Three of the early Derbies were captured by the immor-
tal black jockey Isaac "Ike" Murphy. But after the turn of
the century, black jockeys began to fade from the racing
scene. The last black jockey to win the Derby was Jimmy

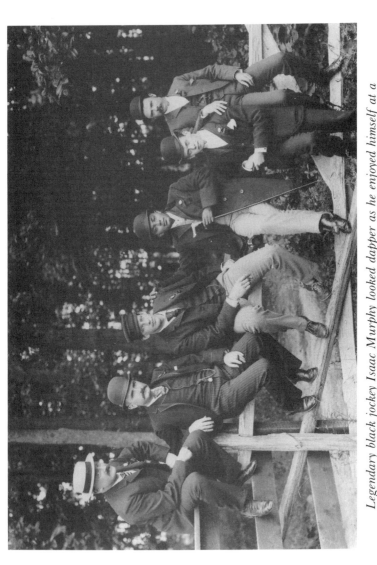

Legendary black jockey Isaac Murphy looked dapper as he enjoyed himself at a nineteenth-century clambake. Murphy rode three Kentucky Derby winners—Buchanan (1884), Riley (1890), and Kingman (1891). (Courtesy Keeneland Library, Lexington, Kentucky)

Winkfield in 1902, and the last to ride in the event was Jess "Long Shot" Conley, who finished third aboard Colston in 1911.

Why have black riders all but disappeared from the limelight of thoroughbred racing?

Roscoe Goose, the late jockey who rode longshot Donerail to victory in the 1913 Derby, once recalled that black riders were squeezed out of their jobs "around about the Twenties, when people got to thinking that if they had a colored boy up, he'd have the worst of it."

The prevailing theory among those who insist there is no discrimination is that blacks are bigger than they once were and can no longer maintain the low riding weight required of jockeys.

Another factor may be that blacks don't have as many opportunities to learn the profession as they once did. A century ago, more blacks grew up on, or around, plantations and farms, and it was only natural that a percentage of them would learn to ride horses and become jockeys. Perhaps, today's black youths, whether they're six-feet-four or five-feet-eight, are more interested in practicing their fallaway jumper than they are in learning how to ride horses.

But basketball hadn't been invented when Isaac Murphy, the greatest of all black riders, was born on a farm in Fayette County, Kentucky. (His year of birth is uncertain; it is listed variously as 1856, 1859, 1860, and 1861.)

Murphy's feats were legendary. He was the first jockey to win the Kentucky Derby three times. He won other major events such as the American Derby four times and the Latonia Derby five times. He claimed to have won 628 of the 1,412 races in which he rode, an incredible winning percentage of .445.

Goodwin's turf guides, available for the last half of Murphy's career, show that during that time he won about 32 percent of his races, an amazing figure.

Murphy was born Isaac Burns, a name he kept until after he started riding. He assumed the surname of his grandfather, Green Murphy, at his mother's request. Isaac's father, James Burns, was a free man who had enlisted in the Union forces and died in a Civil War prison camp.

As a teenager, Isaac was taken by his mother and grandfather to "Uncle Eli" Jordan, a black trainer who began teaching the young boy the art of riding. On May 22, 1875, Murphy launched his career, finishing out of the money in his first race. He started slowly, not scoring his initial victory until the following year, aboard a filly named Glentina. In his first Kentucky Derby appearance, he finished fourth. That was in 1877 on Vera Cruz, who had reared and was left at the post.

Murphy, among the first class of inductees into racing's Hall of Fame (1955), was a great judge of pace. Horseman Jack Chinn once recalled:

"I asked him to ride my horse Ban Fox at St. Louis. It was the time that Bankrupt was sweeping everything before him, and I asked Murphy if he thought he could beat Bankrupt in the race the next day. 'What can your horse go the distance in?' he asked me. I told him he could run the three-quarters—that was the distance—in 1:14½. 'If he can do that, I can win,' said he, 'because Bankrupt can't do it. I have watched the horse closely, and I believe if you head him off, he is a quitter.'

"The next day I took Murphy out and gave him instructions. He was to run the first quarter in :24½, the half in :49 and the three-quarters in 1:14½. Well, I put my trainer at the quarter with his watch and I stood at the half with my own. Bankrupt, as usual, shot out in the lead and Ban Fox followed him two or three lengths behind. As Ban Fox passed the quarter my trainer looked at his watch. It was just :24½. Coming by me, Bankrupt was still well in front and that black machine on Ban Fox was sitting like a log. I glanced at my watch. It was just :49 to the dot. In the last quarter he closed up on Bankrupt, passed him and came under the string an easy winner. I looked at the time when it was hung up. It was just 1:14½."

Instead of punishing his mounts indiscriminately with whip or spur, the gifted Murphy preferred to urge them along gently with his long, muscular arms. Murphy liked to play it close, and frequently he'd ask his horse to give what he considered was just enough to win, a practice that caused the finishes of many of his races to be closer than they should have been. Clearly, a man with a heart problem was better off if he didn't bet on Murphy's horses.

Murphy's first Derby triumph came in 1884 when he rode Buchanan, an unruly horse who had never won a previous race.

Murphy's other two Kentucky Derby triumphs were with Riley in 1890 and Kingman in 1891.

Kingman's Derby was dubbed "The Funeral Procession." The Derby back then was run at a distance of a mile and one-half, and Kingman won in the plowhorse time of 2:52¼, almost eighteen seconds slower than the track record. That 1891 Derby drew only four starters, and every jockey was playing a waiting game as the horses sauntered around the track. Finally, at the head of the stretch, the horses were put into a drive and Balgowan, ridden by black jockey W. "Monk" Overton, moved to the front. Murphy promptly set after him with Kingman. An eighth of a mile from home every jockey—except for Murphy—was whipping away. A sixteenth of a mile from the wire, Murphy then drew his whip and went to work on Kingman, who outfinished Balgowan by a length.

Afterward, Dud Allen, the black trainer and part-owner of Kingman, said, "I know that Balgowan's jockey had been told to go around slow and beat my 'hoss' at the finish. I told Murphy to let Balgowan set the pace and lay for him. I told Murphy to walk if Balgowan walked—and he came near doing it."

Murphy was a man of solid integrity. Unscrupulous turf-men (yes, they existed then, as they do now) learned that Murphy couldn't be bought off, as some riders could, to throw races. "Isaac could have made enough to buy a Blue-grass farm if he would have agreed to lose on Falsetto in the Kenner Stake of 1879," once claimed a man who was close to Murphy.

As another contemporary of Murphy's put it, "The tricksters know too well that no matter how many thousands they might offer, the little brown man with the Spinx-like face would move quietly away and his few words with judges, horsemen, and the public would weigh more than any excuse they could concoct."

Murphy once advised a fellow rider: "Just be honest and you'll have no trouble and plenty of money." Murphy himself made much money during his career. Earning more than fifteen thousand dollars annually during his peak years, he had enough money to buy horses and to purchase a mansion in Lexington near the old Kentucky Association racetrack.

Murphy rode for some of the most influential owners of his era, men such as James Ben Ali Haggin, Ed Corrigan, and E. J. "Lucky" Baldwin. And he rode many outstanding horses during his career, including Emperor of Norfolk, Kingston, Volante, Troubadour, Firenze, and Salvator.

It was aboard Salvator that Murphy won a heralded match race over Tenny on June 25, 1890, at Sheepshead Bay. Tenny was ridden by Edward "Snapper" Garrison, a jockey who was noted for his ability to pull out victories with furious come-from-behind finishes. (Such a closing surge became known in racing jargon as a "Garrison finish.")

Tenny received one of Garrison's powerful closing rides, but Salvator was declared a narrow winner.

From the height of that victory, Murphy plummeted to a

low point two months later in a race at Monmouth. He finished out of the money aboard Firenze, the 6–5 favorite, in the Monmouth Handicap, a race during which the jockey—dizzy and swaying—nearly fell off his mount several times. Afterward, he did topple off. Murphy was charged with drunkenness and was suspended by the judges for an unsatisfactory ride. Murphy insisted that he wasn't drunk but was weak from reducing. Certain observers, meanwhile, speculated that he had been drugged, a contention that Murphy himself later believed.

Murphy fought a weight battle for much of his career. In the off season, he would reach 130 pounds or more, and, as a result, he had to diet to bring his weight down for the races. He was in poor health near the end of his twenty-year riding career, and in 1895 he retired. Less than a year later he died of pneumonia. More than five hundred people, including some of racing's most distinguished personalities, attended his funeral in Lexington.

Murphy left thirty thousand dollars to his childless wife, but his medical bills and debts impoverished her, and she was buried in a pauper's grave.

At the time of Murphy's death, a newspaper obituary suggested that "Honest Isaac" would serve as an appropriate epitaph for Murphy. But only a wooden cross marked his grave, and soon it rotted. In 1909, friends erected a more suitable marker, made of cement. But the cemetery eventually was abandoned, and Murphy's neglected grave was overgrown with grass and weeds.

In 1967, his remains were reburied in a place of honor at the Man o' War Park in Lexington, near the grave of the renowned racehorse Man o' War. "Seventy years from now when I get taken away, you can put me there beside Isaac Murphy," said Eddie Arcaro, who presided at the ceremonies dedicating the reburial of the greatest black rider of all time.

They Started Out at an Early Age

While Isaac Murphy earned plenty of money and glory as a jockey, the average rider—white or black—received little recognition in the old days. Many black riders of the nineteenth century started out their riding careers as young as ten or eleven. Their status was that of stableboys. They learned quickly, and some won the Kentucky Derby while still in their early or middle teens. Alonzo "Lonnie" Clayton was either fourteen or fifteen at the time of his 1892 Derby triumph with Azra, and James "Soup" Perkins was fifteen when he won the 1895 Derby with Halma.

Lightness was the advantage of youth. A newspaper account in 1894 reported that Clayton, a native of Kansas City, could ride at ninety pounds, and that Perkins, of Lexington, Kentucky, could ride as light as eighty-eight. The old-time jockeys often had to be extremely light. Colts were required to carry only a hundred pounds in the first five Derbies, compared with the 126-pound impost that has been the standard since 1920.

When Aristides won the first Derby, his hundred pounds consisted mostly of young rider Oliver Lewis. The black jockey was later to make a name for himself in another area of racing. Working for a bookmaker, he provided detailed information about how horses ran in races and what their problems were. The bookmaker's notes subsequently were developed into the racing charts that served as forerunners of those appearing now in the *Daily Racing Form*.

William Walker was another of the talented black reinsmen of the nineteenth century. Walker, born in 1860 near Versailles, Kentucky, rode Baden-Baden to victory in the 1877 Derby and also was aboard Ten Broeck in that iron horse's triumph over the mare Mollie McCarthy in their celebrated match race on July 4, 1878, in Louisville. Walker rode for some twenty years and then had a successful career as a trainer. An expert on bloodlines, Walker saw every Derby until his death in 1933.

Black jockey Willie Simms had a perfect Derby record, winning both times he rode in the race (Ben Brush, 1896, and Plaudit, 1898). Simms, a native of Augusta, Georgia, also triumphed in such events as the Belmont (twice), Preakness, Suburban, and Champagne.

As a youngster, Simms was "greatly attracted by the gay colors of the jockey's silks at the county fairs," wrote Marjorie R. Weber, the late racing historian. "He determined then and there to become a rider. Without his parents' consent, he set out for New York. . . . In 1895 Simms had three employers, Mike Dwyer, Richard Croker and P. J. Dwyer, who had first, second and third call respectively on his services. His fees for winning mounts, together with his salary, amounted to $20,000. He invested his money wisely and was one of the wealthiest jockeys on the turf."

In the *1987 Kentucky Derby Souvenir Magazine*, Phil Von Borries wrote: "The first American reinsman to win in England, Simms gained notice there for his 'short' style: riding far forward crouched over the neck and the withers, his feet tucked into short stirrups. Though some credit Tod Sloan with introducing the 'short' style to Great Britain, most historians today agree that Sloan only popularized the method and caused it to be permanently accepted. Simms, they say, was the one who showed it to the English turf first."

Jimmy Winkfield . . . the Last Black Jockey to Win

Jimmy Winkfield, born in Chilesburg, Kentucky, near Lexington, won successive Derbies (His Eminence, 1901, and Alan-a-Dale, 1902). Alan-a-Dale was bred, owned, and trained by Maj. Thomas Clay McDowell, who had another horse, The Rival, in the 1902 Derby.

Jimmy Winkfield was the last black jockey to win the Kentucky Derby. He triumphed in 1901 on His Eminence and in 1902 on Alan-a-Dale. (Courtesy Keeneland Library, Lexington, Kentucky)

Apparently there was some last-minute behind-the-scenes maneuvering which resulted in Winkfield's landing the mount on Alan-a-Dale. On the morning of the 1902 Derby, Winkfield wasn't even listed in *The Courier-Journal* as Alan-a-Dale's rider. Nash Turner was.

Years later in an interview with Roy Terrell of *Sports Illustrated*, Winkfield said, "The major had contracted Nash Turner to ride one of the horses and I'd ride the other. Nash was a good jockey, pretty famous by then, and he was a white boy, so he was goin' to get his pick. So for a month I pulled Alan-a-Dale in workouts; I never let him go better than 2:11 for a mile and a quarter, and all the time I galloped The Rival at about 2:09. So when Nash came down on the mornin' of the race, naturally he picked The Rival."

Wink's memory may have failed him a bit in this interview because Turner actually had been in Louisville several days before the Derby, during which time both of the horses worked out. What's more, Winkfield wasn't even aboard either of the McDowell horses when they were given their final serious workouts three days before the Derby. (Alan-a-Dale worked a mile and a quarter in 2:17 on a muddy track while The Rival went slightly faster, 2:16¼.)

According to Turner, his switch to The Rival was a ploy to fool the opposition.

"Switching me to ride The Rival caused Mr. McDowell to win the Derby," Turner said in a post-race interview. "I was put up on the worse horse so as to confuse the other boys riding in the race. They stuck close to me around the first turn, letting Alan-a-Dale set his own pace under wraps. On the backstretch, they still hung to me, thinking I had something up my sleeve. And when I made my move on The Rival after straightening away for home they realized that the horse under me was all out, and the other boys set sail for Alan-a-Dale, but Winkfield had gotten too much of a lead on them. If I had been on Alan-a-Dale, the result might have been different, for Coburn and Williams

("Monk" Coburn and "Tiny" Williams, aboard Abe Frank and Inventor, the other two starters in the Derby) would have chased me hard all the way."

The real reason Winkfield rode Alan-a-Dale in the Derby may never be known, but ride him he did.

The following year Winkfield was seeking a third straight Derby. His mount was Early, the heavy favorite. Winkfield was a genuine star in those days, a rider with considerable ability, but jockeys (particularly black ones) obviously weren't held in high esteem by Jake Holtman, the Derby starter. With starting gates non-existent in 1903, the web barrier was used to send horses on their way. As often happened with web-barrier starting, Holtman wasn't having an easy time getting the horses aligned for an even break in the 1903 Derby. Consequently, he was taking out his wrath on the jockeys, first yelling at one, then another. Just when a perfect start seemed to be in order for the six-horse field, it was ruined because Winkfield suddenly turned Early. In a story that revealed how open racism was back then, *The Courier-Journal* reported the following reaction by Holtman: "'You little nigger,'" yelled Mr. Holtman, whose patience had been thoroughly aroused by this time. 'Who told you that you know how to ride? You are not down at New Orleans now, so come on and get in line.'"

Winkfield finished second on Early, who lost by three-quarters of a length to Judge Himes, ridden by Henry Booker. Booker wasn't particularly fond of blacks either. Rounding into the stretch, Judge Himes went through an opening, and later Booker was freely quoted in *The Courier-Journal* as saying: "Winkfield's arms were hanging loosely, and I thought that Early was fighting for his head. As soon as I got upon equal terms with Early I took special note of his condition. Winkfield turned around at me and laughed. It was then that I was sure that I did not have a chance. That nigger, I was sure, was trying to make a sucker out of me. I thought that he wanted me to come up to him so that he could draw away. I knew that I had all the others beat off, so I just went on. I passed Early. 'I have got that nigger beat,' I said to myself, and then I went to the bat. Winkfield could not catch me . . ."

Not long after an incident that occurred in the fall of 1903 Winkfield left the United States. He had agreed to ride a horse in a stakes for John E. Madden, a prominent horseman, but right before the race the jockey switched mounts so that he could ride the favorite for an owner who had offered him three thousand dollars. A displeased Madden afterward told Winkfield, "If you're not goin' to ride my horses, you're not goin' to ride for anybody." With that, Winkfield decided to head abroad, where he rode in Poland, Russia, Austria, and Germany. Owners for whom he rode included a Polish prince and a German baron. He earned big money—as much as $100,000 a year—before the Russian Revolution forced him to move, and he eventually settled in France. He rode in France and other European countries until he retired in 1930.

Winkfield, who won some twenty-six hundred races during his career, then became a trainer. Returning to the United States during World War II, he went to work on a horse farm in Aiken, South Carolina. Winkfield went back to France in 1953, and in 1974, at the age of ninety-one, he died at Maisons-Laffitte, a suburb of Paris.

Not every outstanding black jockey was fortunate enough to win a Derby. Such well-known blacks as Dale Austin, Tommy Britton, W. "Monk" Overton, Shelby "Pike" Barnes, and Jimmie Lee rode in the Derby, but were unsuccessful. Lee rode in the Derby twice, finishing last both times. He often is listed erroneously as having ridden in another Derby—the 1908 renewal—but he was thrown in an earlier race and a substitute had to ride for him.

Despite his two Derby failures, Lee is remembered for sweeping the entire six-race card at Churchill Downs on June 5, 1907.

When Jess Conley appeared in the 1911 Derby, little did anybody know that he would be the last of a long string of black jockeys to ride in this race. His mount, Colston, was owned and trained by a black man, Raleigh Colston, who had ridden in the first Derby in 1875, finishing out of the money on Searcher. Blacks bet heavily on Colston, who went off at 19–1 odds in the 1911 Derby. As *The Louisville Herald* reported: "Colston had advised his friends to go to Colston and they did."

The newspaper added: "Colston tucked $25 in green in Jockey Conley's boots before the race started, but the mascot failed to work. Had Colston won the Derby we would have been searching for another white man's hope."

The Louisville Herald also reported: "The horse Colston carried the dollar of every dusky hued spectator in the city. Had Colston won there would sure have been some pork chop feasts in town today."

"All Those Boys Were Real Jockeys"—Nate Cantrell

Nate Cantrell remembered well the old-time black riders. A black man who spent a lifetime on the racetrack, he was an exercise boy and assistant trainer. In 1975, still active as a trainer at the age of ninety-six, Cantrell didn't try to hide his feelings in an interview about blacks. He was convinced racial prejudice led to the virtual demise of black riders.

"In the old days, where if you ran twelve horses, from six to eight of the jockeys were always black," he said. "And it remained that way until more money got in the game. Now then when a lot of money got in the game, the white men then, like they do now and like they've always been, wanted his people to have, not only the money, but also the reputation. And that's when they began to pick any kind of a boy that would ride with short stirrups and have a bunch of agents and a bunch of fellas that would canvass around all day and all night to get him on the best horse. And that's how it happened."

Cantrell could remember the old black jockeys.

"I seen Isaac Murphy ride when he comin' in such a close finish when he had to take his whip and put his whip under the chin of a horse and make him throw his head up to win," he said. "He was just that way. I saw him ride, oh, I couldn't tell how many races I seen him ride. I know him personally. He didn't have two words to say to nobody. Everything about him was a gentleman. I don't think Isaac Murphy was ever called in before the stewards twice. Jimmy Winkfield was a little bull-headed one time, but now he was a good race rider."

"Greatest rider I ever seen? Well, you got to give it to Isaac Murphy. I think Isaac Murphy was the greatest race rider ever lived. Isaac Murphy had more ingenuity about him than the average man you could ever speak about. Isaac Murphy, Jimmy Winkfield, Soup Perkins, Lonnie Clayton, and all those boys were real jockeys—were *real* jockeys."

Eddie Anderson (left), better known as Rochester, at Churchill Downs in 1943. (Courtesy R. G. Potter Collection/Photographic Archives, University of Louisville)

15

Celebrities Dreaming of Roses

THROUGH THE YEARS, a handful of celebrities have come to Louisville with hopes and dreams of winning the Kentucky Derby. Comedian Eddie Anderson, popularly known as Rochester on Jack Benny's radio show, was the owner of Burnt Cork, who ran in the 1943 Derby. Band leader Harry James and his wife, Betty Grable, were represented in the 1954 Derby with James Session. Actor Jack Klugman was co-owner of Jaklin Klugman, who ran in the 1980 Derby. And rap star Hammer and members of his family owned Dance Floor, a 1992 Derby starter.

Other celebrities have tried to get horses to the Derby but failed, including Telly Savalas with Telly's Pop in 1976.

And then there was comedian Joe E. Brown, who always joked that the Derby was his "favorite charity." Brown is said to have been a silent partner in the ownership of Porter's Cap, fourth-place finisher in the 1941 Derby. However, his son, Joe L. Brown, once said: "While Dad did have some horses for a few years, and a couple of pretty good ones, to my knowledge none of them ran in the Kentucky Derby. And I do *not* believe that he was a silent partner in the ownership of any horse that ran. He was so enthusiastic about horses that it would have been almost impossible for him to be silent if a horse in which he had a financial interest had run in the Derby. Sorry to spoil a good story, but those are the facts as I know them."

Rochester

"When Mr. Benny called me and said I could go to the Kentucky Derby and take his $50 with me," Rochester said during Derby Week in 1943, "you could have knocked me down with a feather."

As it turned out, the trip to Kentucky was anything but a funny experience for Rochester.

Critics maintained that Rochester was running Burnt Cork in the Derby strictly for publicity purposes, an accusation which the comedian strongly denied.

"The treatment I've received from the press has taken all the pleasure out of my trip here," he said. "I'm entering Burnt Cork in the Derby because I think it has a chance. I'm not here for publicity. Why, we pay $2,000,000 a year to the advertising agency handling our radio program for publicity. I'm too smart a man to make a joke of something sacred to Kentuckians like the Derby for some cheap publicity.

"I respect the reverence with which Kentuckians hold the Derby. My horse has shown by his record that he deserves a chance in the Derby, if the track is right. I mean to give him that opportunity. The race is a sacred thing to Kentuckians—that I know. And just as sacred to me is my obligation to my big horse."

Rochester was advised by many not to run Burnt Cork in the Derby. But one trainer told him, "Listen, Eddie, don't let those dudes train your horse for you. You do what you think best. I've had a lot of horses win—but I've never won a race I wasn't entered in."

Burnt Cork came into the Derby off a last-place effort in the Trial four days earlier. He lost that race by more than forty lengths. But Rochester offered an excuse for this dismal performance, pointing out that the colt had been away from the races for a long time. Burnt Cork had last raced on October 31, 1942, a victory in a six-furlong sprint at Bay Meadows in California.

Rochester was trying to obtain the riding services of Carroll Bierman, who had won the 1940 Derby aboard longshot Gallahadion. "I've offered Bierman a win bonus of $10,000 to ride Burnt Cork," said Rochester. "I hope he accepts because my horse hasn't shown how really good he is yet.

"Don't be surprised," he added with a grin, "if you see him circle the track once and then wait for the rest to catch up, so they can get in the finish picture with him."

Rochester, however, didn't land Bierman and wound up using M. N. Gonzalez as Burnt Cork's Derby jockey.

Many fans made sentimental bets on Burnt Cork, who ran with Bankrupt in a two-horse mutuel field that went off at 21–1 odds.

Just before Gonzalez left the paddock aboard Burnt Cork, Calumet Farm trainer Ben A. Jones went over to Rochester and wished him luck. "We might get second," said Rochester.

Burnt Cork showed early speed but conked out and dragged himself home dead last, thirty-eight lengths behind the victorious Count Fleet.

"He's sure tired, ain't he?" Rochester said afterward.

Tommy Fitzgerald of *The Courier-Journal* perhaps best captured Rochester's post-race mood. "The nutmeg-grater voice of the Benny radio program and the screen was sad, serious and subdued, anything but funny, as he expressed himself hurt by the motives the press ascribed to his starting Burnt Cork in the Derby," Fitzgerald wrote. "And when no vindication was offered in the performance of his Burnt Cork . . . Rochester's chin dropped low enough to shave his whiskers on a blade of grass.

"Rochester either is a good actor or a sincere and misunderstood lover of horse racing."

Fitzgerald wrote that Rochester tried to make himself inconspicuous. "He sought to make himself obscure, but he had as much chance of shedding the identity of Rochester, the funny man of the radio and screen, and assuming the role of the horse-loving, serious-minded Eddie Anderson, the horse owner, as Babe Ruth would have trying to play the part of Gypsy Rose Lee.

"Rochester paid the penalty of fame and publicity and remained the Rochester people laughed at instead of the Eddie Anderson he expressed a wish to be for 24 hours at least—a man who just had a horse running in the Derby. . . . Although he hugged the vicinity of the secretary's office, in the passageway leading from the paddock to the track, until just before the horses went to the post in the Derby, he somehow was as easy to find as a dinosaur in a field of 2-year-old fillies."

Rochester said he guessed that he'd be taking some kidding from Jack Benny and others. "But I don't mind," he said. "I'm not ashamed of Burnt Cork's performance. He was running with the best in America."

Benny did joke about Burnt Cork. On a radio program, a member of the cast said that Rochester intended to ride Burnt Cork back to California.

"He probably would make better time," Benny said, "if the horse rode him."

Mr. and Mrs. Harry James

A newspaper story on Derby Day, 1954, said: "Bill Corum, Churchill Downs president, insists that Betty Grable will be here for the Derby. A box marked 'Mrs. Harry James' was occupied yesterday by a woman who didn't look anything like Betty Grable."

In a 1980 interview, Harry James recalled that neither he nor his late wife attended the '54 Derby.

"I didn't get to go back," James said by telephone from California. "I was working. I had previous commitments with the band. And Betty was doing a picture. In fact, I was in Billings, Montana, the day that the race was run, and I went into a furniture place and I said, 'I'd like to test one of your TV sets out.' So he turned the set on for me, and that's the way I saw the Derby."

James Session, named for a popular recording at the time, finished eighth as a 71–1 longshot. The footnotes in the *Daily Racing Form*'s chart said succinctly: "James Session was outrun."

The '54 Derby was won by Determine, whom James Session had run against in five previous races. Determine held a 3–2 advantage in those meetings.

"We figured we had a pretty good chance," James said, "but when we got back there the horse got sick, plus the fact that the jockey that was supposed to ride him got set down."

James said the only Derby that he had ever seen in person was the 1951 renewal. Count Turf, who was ridden by Conn McCreary, won that race. "Betty's cousin was Conn McCreary," said James. "Conn McCreary was named for Betty's father, Conn Grable. We were playing in Cincinnati that night, and we went down to see the Derby."

James' remembrances of the '51 Derby?

"Well, I remember there were many, many people drinking mint juleps that never did get to see the race," he said. "In fact, there was a guy in front of us in the box that they had given us and this one fella, he was screaming and carrying on, he was singing, 'Old Kentucky Home,' and as soon as the man said, 'They're off,' he fell asleep. That's the truth—right in front of us. It was really comical."

James enjoyed going to the races and playing the horses. "I can't think of anything that I like better except playing music," he said. "I have a pretty good photographic mind for horses the same way I do for music because I can play a tune once and remember it and I can read a *Form* and turn around and remember the post position and where he ran and the trouble he had and everything else. It's just something I'm so interested in and have been for so long a time my mind's adjusted to it."

He said he attended the races "whenever I can—and we still go to Del Mar for our vacation every year. It's just gorgeous."

James owned horses for a long time. He said the first horse he owned was Deviled Egg, who won at a $128.20 payoff at Santa Anita Park on January 18, 1946. "And I thought, oh, this is fun," James said.

James still had horses in 1980, but there was a time that he got out of the racing business. "I was away for ten years because we were working and I really didn't have that much interest," he said. "Then, all of a sudden, I saw a friend of mine. I said, 'Hey, let's get a couple of horses.' So now I got six out here (in California)."

Did James have any racing superstitions? "I think everyone has to a certain point. Like you might go to the same window, the same teller or you might wear the same thing in the box. Just like a ball player, he's not going to change his socks or his sweat shirt if he's hitting. It's the same idea."

Asked if he was rooting for Jaklin Klugman, the horse that was co-owned by actor Jack Klugman, in the 1980 Derby, James replied, "Well, I'm rooting for him. I mean, I haven't met the horse personally, but I think he's one of the nicest men that's ever been in racing. He's the kind of person that we love to have in racing.

"I'll tell you one thing: He'll make a lot of friends because he's a helluva nice guy. You be sure and give him my best and tell him I'll really be rooting for him."

In 1983, the sixty-seven-year-old James died in a Las Vegas hospital. At the time of his death, he owned one horse—Eruptive. A *Daily Racing Form* obituary said: "He had raced horses on a limited scale, primarily at Del Mar, since he and his wife, the late Betty Grable, disposed of most of their thoroughbred holdings by selling 40 head in a complete dispersal at Pomona in 1961. Previously, the two had owned a breeding farm in Northridge, Calif., and later leased the Falk Farm, also in Northridge. After the dispersal, the couple moved to Las Vegas, where they were divorced in 1965. Betty Grable died 10 years ago in the same hospital as Mr. James."

The Jameses bred five stakes winners, racing four of them. Their best homebreds were James Session and Big Noise.

James Session won three stakes races—the Haggin Stakes and the Salinas Handicap in 1953 and the San Vicente Stakes in 1954.

Big Noise, an erratic runner who would race all over the track, captured the 1951 Del Mar Futurity, the 1951 California Breeders Champion Stakes, and the 1952 Berkeley Handicap.

The Blood-Horse magazine reported that when Big Noise triumphed in the Del Mar Futurity, "James was unable to greet him in the winner's circle. His band had an engagement that evening up the coast and in order to be there on time, the leader and trumpeter could not chance getting caught in traffic leaving Del Mar after the feature race. So he parked his car at the top of the hill just north of the track and watched the race from there."

The magazine added that James "had a brief fling as a trainer. Loving the game and wanting to be close to it, he took out a trainer's license at the Pomona County Fair, answering all the questions put to him by stewards with ease. He saddled one winner at the fair meeting, then retired permanently as a conditioner."

A footnote: A broodmare named Miss B. Grable produced sixteen foals (a busy mother, indeed), including a filly with the interesting name of Long Skirts. Miss B. Grable also was the dam of Trumpet King, who ran twelfth as a 106–1 longshot in the 1950 Derby.

Telly Savalas

"We're gonna come your way, my love. We're comin' your way. Watch out. We're gonna make history."

An enthusiastic Telly Savalas was on the phone in 1976, speaking to a Louisville reporter shortly after his Telly's Pop had won the California Derby.

"We've got a legend goin' for us," Savalas went on. "He's somethin'. It's a lotta fun. And the crowds here are unbelievable. He's unbelievable, and it's been a great thrill."

Savalas sidestepped a question dealing with whether or not he bet on Telly's Pop in his races. "He's a 'people's horse,'" he said. "It's not important whether I lose with him, you know—a bet, that is. But what is important is that he satisfies the enthusiasm of the people that come to see him. If you were here today, you wouldn't believe it."

How many people joined Telly's Pop in the winner's circle following the California Derby?

"Uh, the usual 250," Savalas said with a chuckle. "You know, no room for Telly's Pop."

Before Telly's Pop made his next start in the Santa Anita Derby, Savalas relaxed on a couch in a trailer at Universal Studios and talked about his horse during a break from shooting his Kojak television series. "The part of the world (Greece) my people come from we're very flamboyant, we're competitive, okay? And I love the aura of matches and things like that. I don't even know if Telly's Pop is good enough—for anything. I'm going to say he's the greatest. More than that, if I'm going to evaluate the horse, I must do it in a total artistic way and say Honest Pleasure (the Derby favorite) is a great horse. But Telly's Pop is not of this world, okay? He's my own creation in my mind. So he runs one race and I'm dreaming about the Kentucky Derby. That in itself is schizophrenia, right? But it just happens to be coming true. So what I'm doing is perpetuating a legend with a big mouth.

"I'm prepared for Telly's Pop to lose. I'm a realist. I blow bubbles with my kids as well. We're going to go see Telly's Pop win. But I also prepare them for the inevitable. So when he starts losing—if he's going to do it and I hope not 'cause he's such a fun trip—my personality will adjust to that as well."

Telly's Pop hadn't been a winner in all of his races, but at this stage of his career he had triumphed in six of eight starts and earned $343,870. Not bad for a horse that Savalas and his partner, producer Howard Koch, had purchased in an offhand way for a mere six thousand dollars. But Savalas said he wasn't interested in the horse's winnings.

"I couldn't give a damn about the purse money in the Santa Anita Derby," he said. "The purses have nothing to do with it. I'm not into that. But I'm into the festival. I'm into the winner's circle with hundreds of people jumping down because they want to identify with me and the horse. That's a joy.

"I believe in fairy tales. To me, Santa Claus does exist. For those who don't believe in Santa Claus, they bet against Telly's Pop. They're realists. But the dreamers go to bet on Telly.

"He belongs to the two-dollar bettor. He's the people's horse. He's destiny's child. He's a glamour horse."

Savalas said he had brought his father from his home in New York to California in 1975 to see Telly's Pop win a race. "Then he died a couple of weeks later," Savalas said. "I'm glad I brought him out for that because it was a thrill for him."

Savalas had a lot of fun with Telly's Pop, one of the most popular horses ever to race in California.

Savalas claimed that he originally didn't know what it meant when he heard that Telly's Pop was a gelding. "I thought it was a rare kind of color that I wasn't aware of," he said. "Otherwise, I wouldn't have let that happen. I'd rather my horse have fun than run."

Savalas obviously didn't know much about racing, but he was having a ball with Telly's Pop. Whenever Telly's Pop raced, it was "festival time," Savalas said.

Trying to separate fact from fiction with Telly's Pop wasn't always an easy thing to do. Savalas said that he named the horse for his father, but that likely wasn't the case. Koch apparently named the horse after the lollipops that Savalas licked on in his "Kojak" series.

Asked whether he or Savalas named Telly's Pop, Koch said, "What's the difference? Let Telly say that he named him. It sounds better after his father."

Said Savalas with a chuckle: "When I named that horse Telly's Pop, lightning came from the sky, hit that horse in the head and I promise you my old man's running inside him, laughing at us all. And if he blows the Santa Anita Derby I know my pop did that to teach us a lesson. Don't get too cocky, son. Life ain't that way. It ain't all roses."

Telly's Pop was anything but a good-looking animal. When he was led around the walking ring at the Santa Anita Derby, Savalas said, "I can't understand why they call him an 'ugly duckling.' He's gorgeous."

After Telly's Pop ran a disappointing fifth in the Santa Anita Derby, Savalas went to the barn to see his horse. He climbed out of his car, took the wrapping off a lollipop, and, heading into the barn, he asked his daughter, "Is he in a bad mood?"

"No, it's like he's saying, 'Why do people think I should run when I don't feel like it,'" she replied with a laugh.

"What happened, Telly?" Savalas asked his horse. Telly's Pop didn't reply, but Savalas had an answer for a newsman wondering whether the horse still would be pointed for the Kentucky Derby.

"He's going, baby," Savalas said. "He's going. This means *nothin'*. The first time I saw him race, you know, you aim for the things you understand. The only thing I understand is Kentucky Derby. I didn't know nothing about Santa Anita Derby or Hollywood Derby or (pause) San Bernardino Derby. It's the Kentucky Derby. We're gonna run him no matter what."

Savalas wasn't the only celebrity with Kentucky Derby hopes that year. Rod Steiger was co-owner of Stained Glass, and Greer Garson's husband, E. E. "Buddy" Fogelson, owned Thermal Energy.

Stained Glass and Thermal Energy didn't make it to the Derby, but Telly did. The man, that is, not the horse.

Following a sixth-place finish by Telly's Pop in the Hollywood Derby, the horse's Kentucky Derby plans were called off.

But Savalas was among those celebrities in attendance at the Derby. And even though he didn't capture the Derby's gold and glory with Telly's Pop, at least Savalas received a golden lollipop from Kentucky governor Julian Carroll.

"Hey, why don't you try sucking it?" a little boy shouted at Savalas.

Savalas looked over at the youth and said, "Talk to me, will ya? Who loves ya, baby?"

And, baby, who loved Telly's Pop?

Telly Savalas, that's for sure.

Jack Klugman

Take a colt answering to the name of Jaklin Klugman, add a female thoroughbred called Doctor Quincy, and what do you have?

"We call them 'The Odd Couple,'" cracked actor Jack Klugman, co-owner of both horses.

Klugman, who played the medical examiner in the TV series "Quincy M.E." and was the slob sportswriter in the show "The Odd Couple," was talking to a reporter in mid-February of 1980. The Kentucky Derby was still two and a half months away, but Klugman had roses on his mind.

Klugman, who owned Jaklin Klugman in partnership with landscape contractor John Dominguez, was hoping that their colt would measure up to running in the Derby. "The dream is there," he said. "I hope and I pray that it

happens. It'd be the most exciting thing that ever happened in my life. But he's just a damn good racehorse, and
we'll let him tell us where to race him."

Klugman had seen two previous runnings of the Derby.
"I love it," he said. "That's the best week of my life. It's like
Mardi Gras with horse racing, which I love. And I love
Louisville, I gotta tell you. The people are damn nice."

Kentuckians felt the same way about Jack Klugman, who
was a great story leading into that '80 Derby. His horse was
a good story, too, because he was a legitimate contender.
The public might have had the impression that this colt
was a Hollywood fabrication because he was co-owned by
an actor and he had a feminine name. But there was nothing make-believe about Jaklin Klugman. He had done everything good racehorses are supposed to do.

But how in the name of Oscar Madison *did* this colt ever
get a feminine name?

Well, stories differed as to how Jaklin Klugman came to
be named, but Klugman provided this explanation: "My
partner and I have been in horses for a long time. We had
claimed first a sixteen-thousand-dollar horse that came
out of the race lame. It was a gelding so we got about
eleven hundred dollars for him. And then the next day we
claimed a horse for $12,500, The End All. And she came
out of the race lame and couldn't race again.

"They offered us eight hundred dollars for her. My
trainer, Riley Cofer, said to John Dominguez and I, 'Listen, I feel bad about this. I got Orbit Ruler standing, and
I'll give you a free pop. Use her as a broodmare and then
in a couple of years you'll have a foal and you can get five,
six thousand dollars. You'll get some of your money back.'
So my partner said, 'I'm gonna make you *pay* for these bad
claims.'"

Dominguez figured to make his partner pay for the
claims by naming a horse Jack Klugman.

"I said I deserved it because I was picking these horses,"

Klugman went on. "What happened, when it was born they told us it was a filly. So he said, 'All right, we'll call it Jaklin Klugman.' And then I guess somebody turned the horse over about a year and a half later, after we had called The Jockey Club (to name the horse), and said, 'No, no. This is not a filly. This is a colt.' So we were stuck with the name. We figured, well, we'd get a lot of laughs with it."

Laughs weren't all that Klugman and Dominguez received from their California-bred racehorse. Jaklin Klugman provided his owners with plenty of thrills.

He climaxed his juvenile season with a smashing victory in the California Breeders' Champion Stakes at Santa Anita Park. Jaklin Klugman won by nine lengths in 1:20⁴/₅ for the seven furlongs, a full second faster than the stakes record.

The winner's circle resembled a mob scene afterward. As Bion Abbott of the *Los Angeles Times*, wrote, "Jaklin Klugman was responsible for another near record when all the friends of the owners and breeders . . . crowded into the winner's circle, hardly leaving room for the horse. Telly's Pop, owned by actor Telly Savalas and producer Howard Koch, holds the unofficial record for attracting a crowd."

"They say I'm trying to beat Telly Savalas with his crowds," Klugman said. "I got a lot of relatives and friends—plus a lot of people just come down who I know from the track. They figure, 'Well, my buddy won.' And they come down. Dave Johnson, who calls the races, said, 'And here comes Jaklin Klugman into the winner's circle—*if* he could get in.' There wasn't room for him."

As a two-year-old, Jaklin Klugman won four of five races and was ranked at 122 pounds on the Experimental Free Handicap, a tie for fourth. In 1980, he captured three of five races going into the Kentucky Derby, including a head victory in the California Derby and a four-length triumph in the Stepping Stone Purse at Churchill Downs on opening day of the spring meeting.

During his stay in Louisville, Klugman said he was "numb" at being a part of the Derby. "You're here, and you just hope it's real," he said.

Asked about the upcoming Derby, he replied, "I've run it in my mind a hundred times. He's not lost once."

Jaklin Klugman had been foaled on May 3, 1977, and Derby Day came on May 3, 1980. The Derby's fourth choice at 7–1 odds, Jaklin Klugman was eighth the first time past the wire and, rounding the far turn, made a big move on the outside to charge into fourth place after a mile. "Here comes Jaklin Klugman in the middle of the track!" television announcer Dave Johnson exclaimed as the field raced past the quarter pole. Jaklin Klugman moved into second place at the stretch call, and at this point only one horse stood between him and a trip to the charmed winner's circle in the Downs infield. That horse was Genuine Risk, a filly who led Jaklin Klugman by two lengths with an eighth of a mile to go. But the filly wasn't to be denied, and in the final furlong Jaklin Klugman was overtaken by the flying Rumbo. The pride and joy of Jack Klugman wound up third in the Kentucky Derby, losing by just two lengths to Genuine Risk.

Jaklin Klugman had run his heart out, and nobody could ask for anything more.

Later, back at the barn, Klugman was reflecting on the Derby and the game performance that his colt had just turned in. It had been a long day, a long week, and now, an hour and a half following the 106th Derby, Klugman was sitting back in a chair while his colt was being walked around the barn.

Jaklin Klugman was tired from his effort in the Derby, and Klugman himself looked worn out.

A newsman asked Klugman if he agreed with the description of the Derby as the "most exciting two minutes in sports."

Tired as he seemed, Klugman perked up and said, "I would agree with that 400,000 percent. It was fantastic."

"You mean to tell me you're going to sit there and not say it's just another race?" the newsman said, egging Klugman on.

"*What?*" Klugman exclaimed. "Only the bettors say that. That's the greatest two minutes I ever spent in my life."

Klugman praised Jaklin Klugman's effort. "I was pleased as punch," he said. "I mean, he gave every single *ounce* of energy he had—and *then* more. He was magnificent. He was magnificent in defeat, as they say."

"And that's the truth."

Hammer

In the 1992 Derby, Dance Floor represented the Oaktown Stable of Lewis E. Burrell Sr. and three of his sons—Louis K. Burrell Jr., Christopher Burrell, and Stanley "Hammer" Burrell.

Hammer has been no more bashful about betting on his horses than he has been about stepping on stage. For example, the first star to race for Oaktown was Lite Light. In the spring of 1991, she lost the Mother Goose Stakes by a nose to Meadow Star in a stirring battle at Belmont Park, and following that event, Hammer wrote winning owner Carl Icahn a check for thirty-five thousand dollars to cover a gentleman's bet on the outcome of the race.

Following Lite Light's subsequent seven-length victory over Meadow Star in the Coaching Club American Oaks, Hammer said: "It's hard to describe the feeling. It was one of supreme bliss. Ecstasy. It was like watching your daughter running in a race and win after being in diapers. Then she races and wins. Also, I was aware of history being made, being the first Afro-American to win this stakes. It was a great feeling. The credit doesn't go to me; it goes to

Hammer with Marylou Whitney at the 1992 Kentucky Derby. Mrs. Whitney was the wife of the late Churchill Downs director emeritus C. V. Whitney. (Courtesy Benoit & Associates)

my family—to my brothers and my dad. They're the ones that put this whole thing together. I'm just glad to be a part of it.

"We felt very confident. Personally, I felt confident that we would be able to beat Meadow Star. In the last race (the Mother Goose), strategy beat us—bad strategy. I knew it wouldn't be close today. I told the guys at the windows that it wouldn't be close. I asked Icahn if we could make a real bet today. I said let's make it $200,000 today, and I gave him odds on his filly. I gave him $200,000 to his $150,000. All the money is going to charity, to the Help the Children Foundation (in Oakland, California)."

Dance Floor was purchased privately in April 1991 from trainer D. Wayne Lukas with two-year-old colt Rap Master for $265,000. As a two-year-old, Dance Floor won three races, including the Breeders' Futurity by three lengths at Keeneland and the Brown & Williamson Kentucky Jockey Club Stakes by six lengths at Churchill Downs. On the Experimental Free Handicap, he and two other colts were weighted at 119 pounds. Only six males were ranked higher.

Dance Floor opened his three-year-old season with a four-and-a-half length victory in the mile-and-a-sixteenth Fountain of Youth Stakes at Gulfstream Park. He then ran second as the odds-on favorite in the Florida Derby.

Of Hammer, sports editor Edwin Pope wrote in *The Miami Herald* following the Florida Derby: "I never saw a thoroughbred racing owner (a) in such demand for autographs and (b) simultaneously firing such a barrage into the betting windows. Hammer must be the only three-handed folk star alive. He never turned aside a request for an autograph. He walked up to one window and told the ticket seller, 'Keep punching.' Then he tipped her $200. Sign and bet, bet and sign, sign and bet—that was Hammer's Florida Derby afternoon."

In his next start, Dance Floor again failed as the favorite, finishing fourth in the Blue Grass Stakes at Keeneland. His two straight losses, both in mile-and-an-eighth races, led some observers to believe that he couldn't handle the Derby's mile and a quarter. On Derby Day, he went off with Al Sabin (both trained by Lukas) at 33–1 odds.

Writing in *Business First*, a Louisville publication, Billy Reed observed that if Dance Floor should triumph, "the scene in the winner's circle would be the wildest in Derby history, considering that Hammer has been known to observe such occasions by ripping off his shirt and doing a few dance steps."

Dance Floor, breaking from the No. 16 post position, was fifth in the early going before assuming the lead and taking the field through a half mile in :47⁴/₅, six furlongs in 1:12¹/₅ and a mile in 1:37³/₅. At the stretch call, he was third, slightly more than a length off the lead, and at the finish, he was still third, beaten four and a fourth lengths by the winner, Lil E. Tee.

Going into the Derby, Hammer had said, ". . . hopefully you'll see me at the finish line, live and in living color."

Dance Floor wasn't quite able to get the job done so that Hammer could rip off his shirt and do a few dance steps in the winner's circle, but the colt gave his supporters a run for their money in the greatest race of all—the Run for the Roses.